T0159097

THE
HEART
OF A WORD:
The History of Community Hospital East

Daniel T. Miller, PhD

authorHOUSE

AuthorHouse™
1663 Liberty Drive
Bloomington, IN 47403
www.authorhouse.com
Phone: 1 (800) 839-8640

Published by AuthorHouse 09/30/2019

ISBN: 978-1-5462-7650-0 (sc)
ISBN: 978-1-5462-7665-4 (e)

Library of Congress Control Number: 2019900571

Print information available on the last page.

Any people depicted in stock imagery provided by Getty Images are models, and such images are being used for illustrative purposes only. Certain stock imagery © Getty Images.

This book is printed on acid-free paper.

CONTENTS

ACKNOWLEDGEMENTS

This project was only made possible by the support and vision of Scott Teffeteller, Bryan Mills, and Dixie Carter. They were unflagging in their enthusiasm and devotion to preserving the history of Community Hospital East. In addition, the executive team and the support staff of CHE were outstanding in their involvement. Tamara Hartley and Kathy Steffan were vital to the completion of this project. Finally, the people listed below brought their memories of CHE to me in the form of oral interviews and written reflections. All errors belong to the author.

Dr. Rod Corson

Dr. Bill McGarvey

Dr. Jean Mercho

Dr. Bruce Hopkins

Dr. Berj Antreasian

Dr. Don Cline

Venia Hopkins

Deb Smith

Wilma Peacock

Carol Frantz

Anita Harden

Yvonne Shaheen

Judy Northern

Terry Northern

P.E. MacAllister

Dr. Robert Arnold

Jan Bingle

Allen Hicks

Lori Eromyson-Aguilera

Steve Reed

Jackie Means

Mary Brightwell

Bryan Mills

William Corley

John Hague

Dr. William Hilgendorf

Dr. Don Ziperman

Dr. Lou Bojrab

Dr. Larry Monn

Cleo Burgard

Steve Barrett

Paige Dooley

Bill Sigman

Scott Teffeteller

Keith Smith

Dr. John Kunzer

Leonard Betley

Greg Ballard

Willis "Rick" Conner

Gene Sease

Robert Clarke

Allen Wilson

Suzanne Koehler

Donna Curran

Tonya Longwell

Anjanette Wicker

Martha Commodore

Caleb Thompson

Connie Thompson

Karri Amory

Cheryl Mosley

Jill Turner

Kathy Stroud

Mary Conway

PREFACE

"Deeply committed to the communities we serve, we enhance health and well-being." This is the Mission Statement of the Community Health Network.

Who is responsible for providing healthcare services to a community of people? In the mid-1950s the residents and businesses of east-side Indianapolis raised their hands, shared their resources, and collectively established "Community Hospital." That was in August 1956.

For more than 60 years, Community has provided hospital, outpatient, and physician services to this densely populated area (more than 250,000 residents within 5 miles). Additionally, Community has expanded the "communities it serves" to all of central Indiana, including Anderson and Kokomo, both of which also were birthed by the residents of their communities.

Concurrently, Community has become the central Indiana market leader for many healthcare services. This has occurred primarily as a result of its consistent focus on each patient by empowering all Caregivers to treat patients with the same compassion as they would want for their own families. We call this "Patients First" and it is intentionally the first of our PRIIDE Values.

During the past 30 years, east-side Indianapolis has changed. Many businesses, factories, and jobs have gone away. Community Hospital remained but has also aged. Several other healthcare providers have relocated to areas of growth and more suburban populations. Community was faced with a major decision: does it also relocate or does it Reinvest and Reinvent itself on the same site?

Many predicted that Community would follow others and leave east-side Indianapolis. But of course that didn't happen! Community remained loyal to the vision and grit of its founders. It recommitted to its original mission and proudly reopened the New Community Hospital at 16th and Ritter on February 4, 2019!

I believe Community Health Network and each of the Community Hospitals in its Integrated delivery system is the Most Aptly Named Organization. It exists to serve its communities; not only with healthcare services but as true partners in its schools, civic organizations, social services, safety initiatives, churches, economic development, education, and as a good neighbor!

In 2014, Community recommitted its responsibility to the citizen of east-side Indianapolis. Community also committed to research and share the story of Community Hospital. I hope this story inspires each person to renew their commitment and passion to their community.

Bryan Mills
President & CEO
Community Health Network

INTRODUCTION

It was a good year, it was 1985 and I was about to graduate from Indiana Central University, School of Nursing, and really wanted to work at Community Hospital. Nursing jobs were harder to get than they are present day. It was a Saturday morning March and I was all set to attend a new graduate breakfast at Community, being held in the "Salad Bar" area of the hospital.

There were probably 30-40 people there, including the prospective new graduates. We all had an opportunity to introduce ourselves and indicate what area we wanted to work in. A lot of people indicated Emergency room, Obstetrics, or Psychiatry as their top picks. I indicated that I wasn't sure where I wanted to work, but really wanted to get some good experience, any shift, full time. Shortly after the breakfast concluded a nursing director (Karen Pfeiffer) came up to me and said, "I have a great proposition for you, one of my medsurg units is where all the colon rectal surgical patients stay and it is really busy through the week, I have a position that is Monday through Friday, 4 pm to 1:30 am, would you be interested?" Wow! I was totally interested and so my story with Community began, officially June 3, 1985, with my white uniform and nursing cap. Community has provided me with amazing opportunity and mentors that were phenomenal in every way. The leadership at Community has a long-standing history of service, quality (of care and caring) and dedication of which I had great teachers and am proud to carry on that legacy.

I started with Community at it's 30 year/halfway mark and I have seen so much change and growth over the past 34 years. Our purpose is our mission at Community East, deeply committed to the people we serve, we enhance health and well being in so many ways. The greatest part of my career was being part of the executive team that obtained approval from the Board of Directors in August 2014, to reinvest at the East hospital. Since that time, so many wonderful things have happened and we are committed to being at 16th and Ritter for a long time and doing great work, meeting the needs of our community, right where they are.

The story of Community East continues.

CHAPTER 1

A Story To Tell - Toward 1953

"Our family doctor said we need to go to a hospital, but there isn't one around here."

"My children and I have to wait for public transportation to take us to a hospital that is miles away. They're sick and need to go right now. But we have to stand here and wait in this line. I feel so bad for them but there's nothing I can do."

"One of my workers just got hurt on the job. Can't we find a hospital any closer to our shop on the east side?"

"There are more people in this county than any other in Indiana. I'm working hard and trying to raise a family here and yet I can't get access to the care we really need."

Note the words—community, hospital, east.

These expressions came not from people living in a crowded and sprawling 21st century city. No, these were the the feelings and frustrations expressed by people on the east side of Indianapolis and Marion County, Indiana in the first years after World War II.

In the late 1940s, residents of Irvington, Cumberland, Woodruff Place, and other neighborhoods in the area lacked access to a hospital. The eastside's men, women, and children—many of whom, by 1945, had either served or sacrificed in the American effort to help defeat the Axis Powers of Germany, Italy, and Japan—couldn't reach a hospital unless they traveled five miles into the heart of Indianapolis via the electric train system known then as the InterUrban. They had few choices. Accept the unchanging schedule of the train, find some way to drive themselves on bumpy roads, or simply decide not to go to the hospital at all and risk the consequences.

By 1949 a group of doctors in Indianapolis deemed the situation intolerable. Small in number but tight-knit and deeply devoted to caring for the health of families in eastern Indianapolis and Marion County, these doctors had practices in tiny offices along East Washington Street and Emerson Avenue. The doctors were residents as well as medical professionals. That meant that their patients were also their friends, their neighbors, their families.

These physicians included some of the most popular and innovative doctors in Indianapolis. Among them: C.P. Van Meter, the deputy coroner of Marion County and a family practice doctor at a downtown hospital; Malcolm Wrege, a graduate of Harvard and the University of Michigan and fresh from the Korean War as an army medical captain; Paul Kirkhoff, one of the first pediatricians in central Indiana; and Floyd Boyer, a family physician and key leader of the Marion County Medical Society. Not only did they dislike the distance that their patients had to travel—a distance made infinitely longer and more unsettling when a patient was sick or injured—the doctors were dissatisfied at what they viewed as an unnecessary burden of bureaucratic regulations and organizational rules of existing hospitals in downtown Indianapolis. Van Meter and the other doctors recognized that the city's hospitals offered good care. More than that, however, was the desire of the doctors to realize a warmer, more personal atmosphere where patients felt "at home" in every sense of the phrase.

The desire may have sprouted on the east side of the Indiana's capitol city, but it had roots in issues that ran deep in American life of the late 1940s and early 1950s. For the past several months American political figures had been arguing about health care. President Harry Truman had even introduced a nationally-based plan for health care delivery. State and city governments across the US had been debating for more than a decade about affordable health insurance. Added to the mix was the recent habit of employers to offer their employees "health benefits" as a way to avoid wartime bans on increases to wages and salaries.

On top of that, many American cities, including Indianapolis, were poised to cope with choke-points in health care services. There seemed to be too few qualified doctors struggling to care for a rapidly growing population. And perhaps most ominous and unknown of all, urban residents in Indianapolis and elsewhere were fearful of such unpredictable international disasters as atomic and hydrogen war. The local civil-defense shelters established for civilians presented scant protection from unmeasurable carnage.

Linked though it was to larger issues, the problem of a too-distant and too-cumbersome hospital care compelled the group of eastside Indianapolis doctors to seek more than talk, study, and analysis. They wanted action and solutions. To them the way forward was clear: the residents of eastern Marion County needed and deserved a hospital that could provide health care that could be accessed and navigated with ease, speed, and confidence. Van Meter and his medical colleagues sought a place for people to receive major health care services. Even more importantly, they wanted not just *a* people's hospital, but rather *their* people's hospital.

The Van Meter group helped establish a hospital subcommittee within their professional association, the Indianapolis Medical Society. The Van Meter subcommittee and the overall membership of the city's Medical Society circulated petitions throughout Marion County. Nearly 10,000 property-owners, many of them residents living east of Indianapolis, scribbled their signatures on sheets fixed to clipboards. The petitions gave the Van Meter subcommittee and Medical Society the groundswell necessary to form the Hospital Development Association (HDA) in October 1950.

Members of the HDA were Edward Gallahue; Dr. J. William Wright Sr; William H. Book; William Schiltges; James Dunnigan; Dr. Edward Mericle; and J. Dwight Peterson.

Stepping further in the effort, the HDA selected a nationally known hospital consulting firm from Minneapolis, James A. Hamilton and Associates, to sift through population projections, public health statistics, and socio-economic data. Hamilton and Associates also suggested potential action for design and funding.

The HDA also approached the Indianapolis Chamber of Commerce and the Marion County Council before the end of 1950. They agreed to the proposal with an important feature: the funds raised and marked for the effort would not only go toward the new facility outlined by Van Meter and the other eastern Marion County doctors but to several existing hospitals as well. Both new construction and expansion of current buildings would be supported. The centerpiece of the plan, though, was the new facility designated for the eastern portion of Marion County.

The approved plan rested on a bold proposition. Despite a historic number of new hospitals currently under construction around Indiana—many of which relied on funding from the Hill-Burton Act passed by Congress in 1946—the HDA plan would only use privately raised money to pay for the project. No government funds, not from the federal or state levels, would be used. This decision was a powerful first imprint on the identity of the new hospital set for eastern Marion County.

The Van Meter group, Gallahue, and the rest of the HDA confronted a difficult reality. Planning is hard. Executing a plan is harder still. Yet perhaps hardest and most difficult of all is when the plan and execution are both risky and large-scale, two traits that certainly defined the HDA project. That's where the HDA found themselves after securing approval. How to get the money?

The answer rested in the same dynamic that had produced the desire for an eastside Indianapolis hospital in the first place—in the homes and workplaces and community spaces of the people themselves. The people of the area embodied the need for the hospital and so too would they embody the resources vital to making needs and dreams into plans and blueprints. The city's and county's eastside residents would be far more than taxpayers or voters for this venture. They would be, in a very real sense, collaboraters, co-sponsors, and if all went well, co-operators. As a local newspaper columnist put it, the hospital would be "sort of a public charitable trust."

These were uncharted waters.

In late 1951 the original HDA group, along with the Van Meter subcommittee and broader Indianapolis Medical Society, added several key members to their ranks. They included Robert Efroymson, George Kuhn, Charles Lynn, among a score of others that included the mayor of Indianapolis and a handful of county council members. Interestingly, the Association's board included four women. They were Mrs. Alma Bruck, Mrs. Sarah Goodman, Mrs. William Wemmer, and Miss Josephine Madden.

Under the new joined leadership of Efroymson and Gallahue, the expanded group incorporated as the fundraising mechanism for the project. They kept the name used since late 1950 but added a location to define their purpose. The Indianapolis Hospital Development Association opened for its fundraising business on January 12, 1952 at the Indianapolis Athletic Club.

Many of those participating in the Indianapolis Hospital Development Association had served on other vibrant community organization boards such as Goodwill Industries. They often knew each other well from working on behalf of other civic endeavors, such as a post-World War II planning project to guide Indianapolis into the post-war economy. These inter-relationships formed a web of mutual support that could be used to expand the impact of their prior work on the HDA. The inclusion of one such leader broadened access to many other similarly based leaders, whether they were formally involved in the IHDA or not.

The IHDA's board of directors steeled themselves for a long haul. They knew that the simple act of coming together was only the first of many steps. They could not command the residents of eastern Indianapolis and Marion County to open their pocketbooks and their company accounts and donate whatever amount was demanded. The board realized that the people of the neighborhoods would have to be informed, educated, and persuaded to do so. It was a task requiring patience, steadiness, and understanding.

Acting again on the advice of Hamilton and Associates, the board subdivided once more into micro-organizations. For example, a sub-committee emerged which was devoted exclusively to fundraising on the eastside of the city and county. This smaller group—one that was critical to the challenge of tapping neighborhood leadership and energy for the new Community Hospital—was led by John Dunigan. Similar leaders were selected for neighborhood groups closely connected to other aspects of the IHDA's county-wide hospital funding plan.

Both the IHDA and consultants from Hamilton and Associates developed a "speaker's bureau." Volunteers for the speaker's bureau were comfortable with public speaking, often had experience in working on previous civic enterprises such as parks and special celebrations, and could engage effectively with residents in question-and-answer sessions that would be part of speaking activities.

The speakers also utilized carefully chosen marketing slogans and phrases. "Think Big, Start Now" was a phrase emblazoned on signs and posters. "To Save Your Life—You Can't Make A Better Investment" was another popular phrase printed on hand cards and leaned upright on tables where attendees would be seated. "Give Generously To The Hospital Fund" was a clear direction to viewers of an enormous banner and, anticipating the Christmas holiday, "Let's Wrap Up" would captivate audiences in a gift-giving mood.

The speakers' presentations benefited most from displaying an image of the new hospital of eastern Indianapolis and Marion County. Residents weren't asked to donate money for an invisible purpose; the fruits of their labor were there for everyone to see, for everyone to savor and admire.

To design the new hospital, the board chose a well-known local architectural enterprise, Daggett, Naegele, and Daggett. A third-generation family business, the firm had operated since the late 19th century and was located northeast of Indianapolis on Westfield Boulevard at the time when the Van Meter doctors' group had conceived of a new hospital. The firm had a local project list that spanned Jordan Hall at Butler University, the Indianapolis Athletic Club, and the Tabernacle Presbyterian Church.

The architects provided the board and its speakers with more than a sketch or drawing. They furnished them with a unique and creative design, a masterpiece of structural innovation in healthcare. Central to the product was architect James Lewis. He decided that the building should feature an unusual cross layout. The shape of an

"X" would be visible from an airplane. Lewis placed the "X" at a 30 degree angle to true north and south. His placement ensured that every patient room—housing up to 300 patients—would have access to direct sunlight sometime during the calendar year. Each time a member of the IHDA's speaker's bureau spoke to a group in eastern Indianapolis and Marion County, the audience would learn that their new hospital would be anything but ordinary. A place of excellence was about to be built.

The audiences would learn something else, too. Each time the architectural rendering was displayed in a speaker's presentation, it included in gracefully drawn script an unmistakable name: "Community Hospital." This simple title—clear and succinct—captured the spirit of C.P. Van Meter and his band of doctors as well as Gallahue and the original HDA. They would have a hospital of the highest order, done in the name of people who lived and worked together in community.

Finding the right land was as important as having a name and drawing of a building. Charles Shearer and his family owned a 60-acre farm around the juncture of Ritter Avenue and 16th Street in eastern Marion County. The Shearers had owned the land since the early 1900s. A few small houses occupied part of the space now—including the Shearer home—but much of the ground was a blend of trees, bushes, pasture, and swamp. In the daylight old brown grocery bags and tattered newspapers could be seen, the fading papers blown into clumps against the tall weeds. In the dusk, neighbors hunted rabbits or, at night, stalked raccoons in the trees.

It was this acreage that again demonstrated the vital role of Edward Gallahue.

Tall, thin, wearing often a gentle smile and glasses with light-colored rims, Gallahue had just recently celebrated his fiftieth birthday. Gallahue was one of the most unusual business leaders in Indianapolis, perhaps all of Indiana. He was a skilled business man, a brilliant insurance executive, and the organizing force behind the American States Insurance Company, launching the company at age 26 with his brother in 1929. The company began with thirty people. It was less than a year old when the stock market crashed and months later the Great Depression engulfed the United States. Gallahue had guided the business through these harrowing years, a fact which, by itself, testified to his skill. Now, in 1951-1952, American States Insurance had 750 employees, 2000 agents, and had $7.5 million in annual expenses.

The remarkable thing about Gallahue was a restless interest in innovation and creativity. For his company he had built a new office complex across from the Indiana War Memorial on Meridian Street, complete with a large auditorium for both company and community meetings. He maintained a 24-hour per day contact service for all of his customers, and fiercely protected a well-funded employee retirement account to help his workers as they entered old age. Gallahue encouraged his employees to seek additional education and training and to put as much effort into helping the surrounding community as they did his organization. Most especially, Gallahue urged women in his company to seek out leadership positions in professional and community organizations.

Gallahue had an energy and passion for community development that made him a latter-day version of Benjamin Franklin. When with a shortage of nurses that threatened to damage health care delivery in Indiana, Gallahue had worked with local Methodist churches to improve nurse recruitment. When the Children's Museum needed more financial support, Gallahue had stepped forward to be an active fundraiser. When a sudden death struck a board member of Methodist Hospital in Indianapolis, Gallahue agreed to fill the seat at a critical time in the hospital's history. And it was Gallahue who had taken the local interest in a new hospital and other health care improvements and forged it into a new organization, the Indianapolis Hospital Development Association, which had spearheaded the fundraising drive for Community Hospital.

In addition, he sponsored the organization of the Indiana Mental Health Association and was instrumental in bringing two pioneers of mental health care—Drs. Karl and Will Menninger— into the organization. Later, Gallahue launched the world-renowned Menninger Clinic in Kansas, originated a lay leadership program at Earlham College, and collaborated with Princeton University Seminary to establish world religion conferences.

Like Franklin, Gallahue was a leader of many interests, involved in practical solutions to community problems, and knew how to work across different groups and networks. And as Franklin had done with the first community hospital in North America, the Pennsylvania Hospital, Gallahue was determined to help found a new hospital in the community where he lived, Indianapolis.

Gallahue convinced the Shearer family to sell him a portion of their acreage. In turn, Gallahue donated the 28 acres free of charge to the IHDA. Gallahue's donation ensured that not a penny of the money raised was needed to purchase the acreage.

One of the most powerful aspects of the fundraising occurred early in the effort. In Jauary 1953 Mrs. Louise Batties, member of the Indianapolis Mayor's Commission on Human Rights and an African-American civic leader in the city, announced that the prospective hospital—and any other hospital that received these new funds—would be open to all patients regardless of race, religion, or ethnicity. "This represents a great forward step," declared Batties. The announcement ensured that the new hospital in eastern Marion County would be built on a principle of racial equality.

As 1953 unfolded, fundraisers urged potential donors to think about specific places inside the proposed Community Hospital. People could now give money toward an exact location in the future building. "Because it is a nonprofit voluntary hospital concerned only with humanitarian service and because it has been made possible only through giving," as a public handout described it, "it offers ideal opportunities for the establishment of individual Memorials. Every room, every piece of equipment, every item of furnishings, offers an opportunity for a Memorial."

The call for funds rang forth at exactly the time of economic vibrancy in eastern Indianapolis and Marion County. New companies had arrived along major roads and streets east of downtown Indianapolis. Existing companies had expanded their operations to an impressive degree. The city's first "interstate exchange", located on Shadeland Avenue, carried workers to and from massive new manufacturing and transportation plants with names that dominated American industry—Ford Motor Company, Western Electric, International Harvester, Chrysler, Naval Avionics, and many others. Like mushrooms after a spring rain, dozens of smaller support companies suddenly popped up nearby, offering services and supplies to these enormous customer-plants.

The vast majority of these employers eagerly signed on to the Community Hospital campaign. Their workplaces became donor-places. Employees filled their parking lots, meeting rooms, lunchrooms, break areas, lobbies, and even assembly lines whenever public speakers, materials, and conversation turned to the issue of raising hospital funds. Bookkeepers and accounting departments sent paycheck envelopes with information about the proposed hospital and fundraising. Employees agreed to have a percentage of their wages deducted from each paycheck for the hospital fundraising campaign. Mid-level managers and supervisors organized contests to see who could raise the most money. The latest entertainment technologies were popular prizes for winning fund-raising groups in these workplaces: one group of workers earned a new television—an unheard-of luxury in most homes—and another group won a clock radio, a newly introduced item in the consumer marketplace.

Local businesses and residents rushed to give money for a specific part of the proposed hospital. The Murat Temple gave money for operating rooms, bedrooms, and furnishings. The Efroymson family donated thousands of dollars for items to fill up entire floors of the hospital; other families followed with more modest amounts. Diamond Chain paid for a family room, while RCA, Stokely Van Camp, AUL Insurance, Vonneget's Hardware, and International Harvestor sponsored waiting rooms, patient rooms, and more. Merchants National Bank and Trust underwrote the pharmacy. Indianapolis Life donated a birth delivery room, and individual patient rooms were supported by Farm Bureau Insurance, the American Legion, and Indianapolis Power & Light. The Indianapolis Star and Indianapolis News donated more than $100,000 that went toward various items on the list. The roster of donors was exhaustive.

At the bedrock level of the area, however, was one of the most important groups of all, the Irvington Union of Clubs. This group was an influential and prestigious organization in Irvington, a small yet vibrant community east of downtown Indianapolis on Washington Street, or the Old National Road, near the medical practices of Van Meter and the other activist doctors. Founded in 1926, the Irvington Union of Clubs had a network of twenty-nine organizations that worked in the arts, education, health, and contemporary social trends. These groups were well-versed in complex issues, having convened recently to listen to a nationally known economist and industrial consultant discuss "We Can Save America." Members of the Irvington Union of Clubs were thoughtful and insightful people.

They had turned out in droves to hear some of the first presentations on the proposed Community Hospital. Convinced of the need for the facility, the Union's members quickly organized a women's group, led by Mrs. Alma Bruck, an Indianapolis school board officer and Irvington leader. Bruck gave them the name of Women's Auxiliary of Community Hospital and it stuck. Like the employers, the Irvington Union of Clubs and the Community Hospital Auxiliary generated both enthusiasm and money for the project.

The Irvington Union of Clubs added to the momentum seen in the fundraising activities of eastside employers. Motivated by what they described as "Indianapolis's greatest civic endeavor," Club members often had families working for these same employers and many had spouses or siblings in executive and upper managerial positions. They went house-to-house, street-to-street, block-to-block, knocking on doors and encouraging young and old, men and women, white and black, newcomers and long-timers, homeowners and renters alike to donate whatever they could to the proposed Community Hospital.

A dazzling array of events kept the momentum going. Music was a must; dances, singing contests, and shows were organized. Events featured audience members who had strong singing voices; anyone could stand behind the steel-rod like microphones and sing a tune of their choice. At the Columbia Club, older crowds swayed to the music of Frank Sinatra, Tony Bennett, and Perry Como, while in community halls and high schools younger participants danced to Fats Domino and Bill Haley. Local professional musicians contributed their talents to these events as well; the Indianapolis Symphony Orchestra held a special concert with Russian-born Fabien Sevitzky conducting, while a popular black quintet performed favorite jazz tunes at another concert. The Rotary Club sponsored the comic opera "Mikado" and gave the proceeds to the hospital fund.

If you couldn't sing or didn't want to dance, there were other ways to donate and raise money for the hospital. Movie-goers were able to attend a movie at one of fourteen theaters and had the cost of their tickets slated for the hospital. Those who enjoyed writing were able to compete for prizes in essay contests. People purchased raffle tickets or played bingo to win prizes. Others donated used clothes, toys, and furniture for "rummage sales" to raise money. And if eating or cooking was your skill, pitch-in meals were a popular way to draw a crowd and seek donations.

There were more somber events, too. With tensions between the United States and Soviet Union at dangerously high levels, one social club organized a fund-raising event around a speech on "Americanism." The employees of West Baking Company honored one of its co-workers—Sargent Major Gilbert Albert—who was killed in the Korean War with donations made to the hospital in his name. By any and all means people came together to learn about the proposed new hospital and have the chance to donate money toward the project.

Symbols of the fundraising came into view. Buckets, baskets, cans, and jars were often the most common way in which the people of eastern Indianapolis and Marion County pooled their money. In coins, dollars, and checks, they collected money in these modest containers found in homes, garages, and tool sheds. The simplicity of the receptacles underscored the nature of the fundraising itself.

As important as the money was the mood in which it was given. People smiled, laughed, nodded seriously, shook hands earnestly. They sang songs, shouted cheers, recited poems, and told stories. Later in life, adults would look back on childhood, living in the neighborhoods of Marion County's east side and recalling a parent, a grandparent, an aunt or uncle who added hard-earned dollars and cents to the growing coffers of money. Before the first shovel of dirt was turned, the spirit and substance of what they did laid a foundation for the hospital to come.

"This drive," a participant asserted, "will obviously go down in history as the swiftest, most effective fundraising campaign of our time," and shows, said another, "what a community can do without Federal aid."

Because of what they did, this was a story to be told and re-told.

CHAPTER 2
A Founding Stream, 1952-1955

The story of the fundraising to build and launch Community Hospital was genuinely remarkable. Within that story, however, were especially significant moments with implications for the future. Long before the structure was built, a different kind of foundation was being laid. An identity and purpose formed within the idea of Community Hospital.

The first boost to the campaign occurred in April 1952. Robert Efroymson, chairperson of the board of directors for the Indianapolis Foundation, announced that his organization would donate $200,000 to the drive. It was the opening major gift of the campaign and, up to that time, the largest single donation in the foundation's 36-year history.

Efroymson was the Jewish son of a Jewish mill owner; his father's company had produced hosiery and clothing for soldiers who had worn parachutes in World War II. Efroymson's father was also instrumental in founding one of the first community foundations in the United States. Robert Efroymson had not only taken on his father's duties at the clothing company and the community foundation but expanded his business to investments and capital finance. He was also active in community affairs and, like Gallahue, crossed over gracefully into causes and projects beyond business dealings. Efroymson quickly became a leading voice for Community Hospital.

Another momentous donation was from Eli Lilly & Company. Vice

President Charles Lynn announced that the pharmaceutical company, in tandem with Lilly Endowment, would contribute $1.2 million, a full ten percent of the targeted goal. Lynn was a major transformative force at the company and had several deeply held personal interests that related to community affairs, including religion, public nursing, animal health, and the beauty of the English language. By the time Community Hospital would see its first patient, Lynn would earn a special commendation from the Queen of England for his work on promoting Shakespeare and other English authors.

The impact of these donations echoed across the region. George Kuhn of the Indianapolis Hospital Development Association said it "was the good old Hoosier way without going to the Federal seats of government where they'd tell us how many hospitals to build." Kuhn co-owned a major commercial realty firm in Indianapolis who linked the fundraising drive to countless business and civic leaders throughout Indianapolis. A friend of Kuhn's, Willis Conner Jr, vice president of Merchants National Bank and Trust and general chairperson of the hospital's fund drive, asserted, "It emphasized that Indianapolis citizens are thinking in proportion to the magnitude of this program."

Conner was a fixture in Indianapolis economic and civic life. He was a vice president at Merchants National Bank. Extroverted and fascinated by people, he'd served as chief fundraiser for the 1950 campaign of Indiana Red Cross and before that was executive director of Indiana's War Finance Committee during World War II. It was a short step for him to emerge as the public face of the hospital fundraising campaign. He was inextricably joined to either its success or failure in amassing a target amount of $12 million, the largest chunk of which was slated for the new building. As far as the overall fundraising was concerned, it was Conner who put his personal reputation on the line for the proposed Community Hospital.

In late 1952 the Council organized one of its most popular events of the campaign. A national radio and movie celebrity, Jean Hersholt, was the featured speaker at the Scottish Rite Cathedral in Indianapolis. Born in Denmark, for more than twenty years Hersholt had starred in a weekly radio program (directed by Neil Reagan, brother of the future American president) as "Doctor Christian", a wise and kindly physician in a fictitious Midwestern town, River's End. Hersholt was so beloved in the public mind that he received hundreds of letters asking for medical advice. He had turned his popularity to serious ends, organizing a fund for actors who needed medical care but couldn't afford the costs. Hersholt was thus the perfect choice to speak with passion and eloquence to Indianapolis residents about donating their money to the proposed new hospital.

Hersholt spoke to nearly 2000 people. "We must realize that we cannot depend on a paternal government or luck to take care of us," Hersholt intoned. He emphasized the vital need for the project and celebrated local support for the fundraising. Using humor to underscore his point, Hersholt joked, "I've operated for sixteen years without a shingle." The night ended with the Indianapolis Medical Society awarding Hersholt an hononary medical degree and General Motors Corporation donating $1 million to the project.

A week before Christmas in 1953, the target was hit, the goal was reached. It was a staggering achievement. More than 7500 volunteers had collected $12 million from 110,000 people to build the new Community Hospital and to expand Methodist and St. Francis Hospitals.

The Indianapolis Hospital Development Association (IHDA) convened a press conference on December 18, 1953 to announce the accomplishment. So began the first of three important ceremonies in making the idea of Community Hospital into more than a building.

The event highlighted four members of the IHDA. Willis Conner, Jr, George Kuhn, Edward Gallahue, and Charles Lynn stood behind a table holding formal scrolls that had been fashioned for them. The scrolls were in recognition of their work for the past thirteen months.

In addition, though, the four leaders were the recipients of a special letter from US President Dwight Eisenhower. Eisenhower wrote the letter with the expectation it would be read aloud at the press conference. According to Eisenhower, "Excellent organization, rare diligence, and a warmly responsive citizenry" were all evident. "It was a stirring example to all citizens everywhere who are striving for the improvement of their respective communities," he added. And the missing element was the key for, as Eisenhower concluded, the project was done "without the participation of Federal or local government."

These sentences were significant. Eisenhower was the first American president since the late 1920s to have emphasized a return of state and local power in balance with federal power. He was eager to show an alternative to the large-government and massive federal spending embodied in the presidencies of Franklin Roosevelt and Harry Truman. Though Eisenhower believed deeply in the strength of the federal government for national security and large-scale public projects like Social Security and the emerging "interstate" system, he hoped to champion a new, common-sense approach of public support and private involvement. The Community Hospital project was among the clearest examples—one of the few—of re-balancing national and public-based power in the mid-1950s.

Conner, Kuhn, Gallahue, and Lynn smiled at each other. With the simultaneous sound of "click-and-pop," a photographer captured the scene with echoes of Eisenhower's letter fading in the air. For Indianapolis it was truly, an observer said, the "greatest Christmas gift in community history."

With the goal attained, mundane issues came to the fore in 1954 and 1955. Fundraising for Community Hospital continued. A minor problem was the occasional gap between people's pledges and their payments. The enthusiasm of promising to give sometimes faded in the harsh light of savings accounts, check books, and real revenue. With tact and care, though, money came steadily in. As it did, Robert Efroymson, Edward Gallahue, and the Indianapolis Hospital Development Association poured over construction bids for the building projects. By late August 1954—at the same time President Dwight Eisenhower signed a law banning the Communist Party in the United States—the group selected Huber, Hunt, and Nichols to do the work.

Despite the routine tasks, big plans were in the offing. Indiana's 11th district congressman, Representative Charles Brownson, and Indianapolis Chamber of Commerce vice-president, William Book, hit upon the notion of inviting US Vice-President Richard Nixon to a ground-breaking ceremony for Community Hospital. Nixon replied hesitantly, stating he had nearly filled his speaking calendar for the rest of the year. Willis Conner delayed setting a ground-breaking date so as to keep the option open for Nixon to attend.

The delay worked. Nixon finally agreed to participate and the date for groundbreaking was set for September 23, 1954. It was a Thursday and the first day of autumn, though at 80 degrees the summer still lingered over the gardens and corn fields of central Indiana. Indiana's Governor George Craig declared, "It is appropriate that the Vice President is coming here to break ground for a hospital that will become a monument to unselfishness and ingenuity of Indianapolis citizens."

Richard Nixon's appearance fit within the broader congressional election campaign of 1954, the first for President Dwight Eisenhower elected two years before. Nixon had campaigned actively for Republican candidates for the US Senate and House of Representatives across the nation. To his supporters, he was a no-holds-barred speaker, to his opponents an attack-dog, but in either event Nixon was the most forceful and aggressive of Eisenhower's campaigners. It was a role he relished. He had decided to participate in the groundbreaking ceremony because he could also speak at an election rally later at Butler University's Hinkle Fieldhouse.

Nixon arrived in Indianapolis by special plane from a campaign stop in Duluth, Minnesota, in the early afternoon of September 23. From the tarmac at Weir Cook Airport, a driver and escort led Nixon to downtown Indianapolis. An excited contingent of Marion County Young Republicans, led by Keith Bulen and Barbara Corbitt, greeted Nixon. He joined a well-organized caravan of cars, many of which were convertibles with the tops down on this hot and sunny day. Nixon had asked about using a convertible but Indiana police refused his request because of safety concerns. Throngs of people lined Washington Street on the five-mile route from Monument Circle to Ritter Avenue.

Paper confetti poured out of office windows and rooftops onto the Nixon caravan. Each piece flickered in the sunlight, the tiny shadows floating and drifting through the air. At one point, hundreds of thin strips of paper draped over Nixon's right arm as he leaned out the backseat's passenger window to greet the crowds. Nixon wiped the streamers from his arm before the caravan arrived in the Irvington neighborhood.

Once to the Ritter Avenue intersection, Nixon saw red-white-and-blue buntings hanging from storefronts and American flags hanging from lampposts. He smiled again at the people lined three and four deep on either side of Washington Street in Irvington; school children were especially visible, having been released from classrooms in order to see the Vice President on this special day. They cheered Nixon, who waved warmly back at them. Members of the Irvington Chamber of Commerce beamed with pride at the scene.

A special platform awaited Nixon in an open field at 16th Street and Ritter Avenue. Politicians, business executives, religious officials, key fundraisers, local leaders, and more stood on the platform, while a large crowd formed behind a short wooden barricade. Beyond the crowd was a row of small houses and cleared ground. The raccoons and rabbits were gone.

The program began with prayers, songs, and welcoming speeches. Nixon heard powerful phrases from Christian and Jewish leaders: marking "the industry and enterprise of the city and its neighborly concern for the weak and afflicted"; "a haven of healing and a mending place for the souls of men"; and "we stand on Holy Ground and God's presence is in our midst."

By 3:45pm it was Nixon's turn. He walked to the podium in front of a cheering crowd. Lean and fit, dressed in a dark suit, he looked out over hundreds of people, a row of small houses behind them. Reading from notes and glancing occasionally out at the audience, Nixon attempted to draw the crowd to him. He asked those in attendance to remember he was one of them after all, the son of a Hoosier mother. Then, he began to praise the people of Indianapolis, Marion County, and Indiana for their valiant effort in raising money for the new Community Hospital.

As Eisenhower had done with his letter months before, Nixon fixed the new hospital to a larger story. He reminded the crowd that he didn't normally attend events like this one—"usually, it is a Federal project I dedicate." "This is different," he noted, "I have come here to dedicate a project typical of this city and this state. This hospital will stand in tribute to your self-reliance." He added, "It shows the true Hoosier spirit."

Nixon elaborated on the greater meaning of the project. The effort symbolized the good produced when "states and local communities do as much as possible for themselves." Some communities simply couldn't replicate what had occurred here in Indianapolis, Nixon admitted. They often didn't have the resources or assets to make it work. In those cases, he said, the federal money saved here would be used by the federal government elsewhere, in those places unable to follow the example of Indianapolis and Community Hospital.

Intriguingly, Nixon's speech had tempered Eisenhower's letter. Eisenhower had held up the project as a showcase of an alternative to the large, public-sector, federal-government planning of Franklin Roosevelt and Harry Truman. Nixon agreed wholeheartedly with Eisenhower, yet also chose to hint cautiously at the likely limitations of Community Hospital as a national model. Nixon's interpretations of the event suggest that this was a unique place, a unique enterprise, a unique set of conditions, a unique founding. It was, at root, a unique identity.

Slightly after 4pm, it was over. The crowd applauded loudly for Nixon's speech, the people on the platform shook hands and congratulated each other, and the marching bands sounded their final notes. Nixon returned to his motorcade and then back to the Columbia Club on Monument Circle. Later that night, he gave a fire-eating political speech at a rally at Butler University's Hinkle Fieldhouse.

During the weeks and months that followed, workers quickly began to build Community Hospital. Board chairperson Robert Efroymson asserted the construction was "well underway and progressing as rapidly as practicable." Local realtors adapted to the new presence of the structure by emphasizing in home advertisements that a particular house was near the "new Community Hospital."

By summer 1955, the board of directors organized another special ceremony. The purpose was the laying of the new Community Hospital's cornerstone. It was an act that symbolized everything at the core of beliefs among the hospital's founders, fundraisers, and general public who supported the facility. This event, much like the ground-breaking and the Nixon speech of the year before, defined the birth of the organization.

The organizers chose and planned carefully. Rather than politicians or celebrities, they picked one of their own to share the principles, dearly held, that would characterize the new Community Hospital. For the challenge of bringing the unbuilt hospital to life, for weaving a future from the materials of past and present, they turned to Mrs. Alma Bruck.

Confident and proven in her leadership, Bruck seized the moment. She was skilled at public-speaking and steeped in intricate topics like local and neighborhood identity. Bruck crafted a theme that struck at the core of the new Community Hospital. She wrote and re-wrote a speech around the concept of "Hospitals are People." Bruck's goal was to explain the "role of the community-built and community-operated hospital." She viewed her remarks as defining the entire ceremony. Bruck's address would follow the path set by Eisenhower's letter and Nixon's speech.

Bruck, Efroymson, Gallahue, and the rest also wanted a special symbol at the event to encompass everything they envisioned for the new Community Hospital. They decided on a time capsule. They picked a stout copper box to protect, in their provocative phrase, the "mementos of our civilization." The copper box would hold cherished items that gave meaning and tangibility to speeches which would disappear into the air. Like seeds into soil, they would implant the copper box in the hospital's cornerstone.

Community Hospital's copper box and cement cornerstone hinted at a further reality that later generations would easily overlook. The IHDA and local supporters of Community Hospital feared that the box and cornerstone might have to withstand the blast of atomic and hydrogen bombs. Residents of Indianapolis were updated on an almost weekly basis of likely bomb-based war between the United States and Soviet Union. These bombs would rain down on Indianapolis and other American cities. So serious was this fear that Indianapolis Mayor Alex Clark ordered the cleaning up of vacant lots because dead grass and dried litter would fuel the fires started in the likely explosions over the city. The workers building the new Community Hospital were thus doing simultaneously two tasks vital to the city—building a new hospital after cleaning the ground to reduce atomic catastrophe.

Given the weight of the occasion and the circumstances surrounding it, Gallahue, Efroymson, Bruck, and the entire group devoted careful thought to selecting items for the copper box.

Two sources filled the capsule. The first was the fundraising campaign, especially the role of local people and organizations, the fanfare of public participation that had energized an entire city. They collected black-and-white photographs of the fundraising effort, including images of checks awarded, gatherings organized, and speeches delivered, Nixon's included. These were frozen moments of the good and happy times, of people united to do the right thing and launch the new Community Hospital.

The second source was quite different. Members of the IHDA board collected specific editions of local newspapers, the Indianapolis Star and Indianapolis Herald. These newspapers, spanning the recent months down to the date of the ceremony, detailed the real-life story of polio in Indianapolis, one of the most dreaded diseases of the mid-20th century. Entire families in Indianapolis—and every other city in the United States—worried over the prospect of a family member, typically a child, succumbing to the affliction and its lifetime of metal-bracketed legs and perpetual immobility. Citizens could recall President Franklin Roosevelt and his polio as well as the anti-polio organization, March of Dimes, known in nearly every neighborhood.

Folded and tucked into the copper box, the newspapers depicted a ragged and raw challenge in dealing with polio in Indianapolis down to summer 1955. Journalists in the newspapers described the work of research scientists Jonas Salk who had discovered a vaccination for polio two years earlier. The journalists also wrote about the valiant efforts of local pharmaceutical company, Eli Lilly & Company, one of Community's major donors and a key entity in manufacturing the drug for mass distribution. The articles included commentary on resistance to the vaccination, the squabbling and divisiveness born in a volatile and uncertain flow of events. The breadth of the articles laid out the reality of a community coming to grips with danger, risk, duty, controversy, and innovation in a public health crisis. The clear signal was that, in a future moment, the new Community Hospital would be not only involved but a leader in collective action and direct response.

To deepen the impact of the issue, the board members placed a glass vial of Lilly's polio vaccination into the copper box.

They also added to the time capsule a Lilly-published book on medical history, innovations, and terminology; medical magazines; and a handful of new medical devices. To finish it off, they laid a carefully folded American flag, made of strong, thick fabric and complete with 48 stars, one for each state in the national union. Then they sealed the copper box shut.

For all the planning of this important day, the board members forgot one thing: the weather. A downpour of rain washed out the ceremony in late July 1955. The organizers improvised the next step. Aside from informing newspapers that the ceremony had been cancelled, they ceased further celebration. Instead, they contacted the construction crews working to build the hospital and asked them to insert, privately and without publicity, the copper box into the cornerstone. Taking a break from digging in the dirt, from pouring and forming cement, from moving rocks and laying stone, the tired workers buried the copper box.

The task done, both the workers and the boards got back to the business at hand.

Taken together, these ceremonies of 1952-1955—the announcement of shocking large donations and local support; the Dwight Eisenhower letter; the Richard Nixon speech; the planned but canceled Bruck address; and the filling of the copper box—constitute what might be called the founding stream of Community Hospital. They were multiple events, separate but joined, shared by and moving with many of the same people along the flow of time. Before any patient had been treated, before any light had been turned on, before any person was employed, these events had imprinted an identity on the entity called Community Hospital.

CHAPTER 3
Down To Work, 1956-1959

At some point, even the best and most noble purpose must get down to business. Idea and aspiration become reality and work. Spirit gives way to sweat. An organization must be formed and jobs must be done.

For Community Hospital, an important challenge began in August 1956 that, in many ways, would have no end. That's the time when the front doors swung wide to welcome visitors and guests, staff and patients. The challenge was to ensure that the cause of Community Hospital would become the culture of Community Hospital.

Community Hospital was the scene of an "open house" on the weekend of August 3-4, 1956. The open-house accomplished two things. It expressed gratitude to those who had given money and time in building the hospital, while it informed those who would use a hospital that this place was in fact ready to receive patients. And in numbers that astounded even the event's most optimistic planners, the people poured in on that hot summer weekend.

312 hostesses welcomed more than 17,000 people into the new Community Hospital. They streamed in not only from eastern Marion County and eastside Indianapolis, but also from nearby Hancock, Hamilton, Shelby, and Johnson Counties and from outside central Indiana. Guests from other states came, too, doctors, nurses, hospital officials, and business owners and executives, politicians, ministers, and on and on. Leaving their names, addresses, and hometowns in

leather-bound notebooks, they came to see what had been done at the new hospital on the corner of 16th Street and Ritter Avenue.

Many of them visited as families. Dad, Mom, and kids all clustered together. A young girl named Debbie asked her parents: "where do the patients stay at night?" Upstairs, in the patient rooms, they gazed at modern, creative decor, especially "the tawny cherry and contempoary styling with draperies of printed sailcloth floral patten, harmozing with the wall colors." The young girl named Debbie was so impressed that she began thinking about finding a way to spend more time at the hospital.

At 10am on Monday, August 5, 1956, Community Hospital's first patient arrived and was admitted. She was Emma Nicoll, 81 years old, a member of the Irvington Presbyterian Church. Excitedly, the front-lobby staff escorted Nicoll to her room where nurses had gathered. Actual healthcare at Community Hospital had now begun.

The facility with its first patient was a place of innovation, a center of excellence. Described by a newspaper reporter as "an ultra-modern hospital," Community Hospital offered exciting innovations to incoming patients like Emma Nicoll and her family as well as to physicians and staff. These innovations were visible even from the street with the building's unique "X" design. Upon entering the facility, the color scheme of the painted walls was bright and cheerful. Pillars of Vermont stone and paneling of East Asian mahogany caught the attention of many people who entered the hospital lobby; it was the type of material ususally reserved for museums, government buildings, and wealthy homes. The surroundings signaled to Emma Nicoll and other eastside residents that they could be proud of their new Community Hospital.

In addition, the facility featured designs meant to promote personal comfort and labor-saving techniques. Hot and cold water flowed through a piping network that produced air-conditioning in Nicoll's room and every other room. Community Hospital was the first in Indiana and one of the first in the Midwest to have this system. Oxygen also flowed into most patient rooms, thereby eliminating the heavy tanks that contained the precious element in ordinary hospitals. In case Nicoll needed surgery, Community Hospital's operating tables had the capability of being adjusted from a single position, while dumbwaiters and pneumatic tubes carried supplies from a central location to Nicoll's floor and throughout the building.

A wired telephone system ran to not only Nicoll's room and every patient room but through every level as well. Every square foot of the five-story structure belonged to a vast communication network. In an age that saw the Soviet Sputnik satellite shock Americans across the United States, Community Hospital on the eastside of Indianapolis introduced a degree of connectedness that set the standard for healthcare in the mid-1950s.

Emma Nicoll entered a hospital that was already bearing the mark of two particular people. They were crucial to the transition from ideas and plans to work and execution. To Emma Nicoll and the thousands of patients who followed her, the imprints of Wilbur McLin and Mrs. Alma Bruck would be deep and lasting to Community Hospital.

With the word widely circulated of the emergence of the new Community Hospital, hundreds of applications flowed in to Robert Efroymson and Community Hospital's board of directors for the position of superintendant, or chief executive officer. Efroymson and the board knew that the hospital's formal leader, the person whose face, image, and reputation would be inextricably linked with the hospital in the public mind, would set the tone for the rest of organization.

They chose forty-four year-old Wilbur McLin, the first employee of Community Hospital. With dark hair that he kept trimmed short, McLin was thin and wore wire-rim glasses in front of narrow eyes. His face bore the trace of a faint smile and a thoughtful look. McLin was studious, ambitious, and blessed with a background that fit well with the challenge of opening and operating a unique hospital.

Born in 1912, McLin was raised in central Iowa. He was a graduate from the University of Iowa. He majored in business administration and excelled in financial analysis of trade, commerce, and industry. After the United States entered World War II in 1941, McLin had entered the nation's military as a second lieutenant in the Medical Administrative Corps, thus beginning a shift into a lifelong world of healthcare and economics. He ended World War II with the rank of major, serving twenty-seven months in the European theater.

McLin was a decorated medical officer; he took home the American military commendation of the Bronze Star and the French military award Croix de Guerre. By 1945, he was back in Iowa as assistant superintendent at the University of Iowa hospital.

McLin left Iowa after only a year for another assistant superintendency, at Jewish Hospital in Cincinnati, Ohio. Just twelve months later, he moved again to yet another assistant superintendency, this in Indianapolis at Methodist Hospital. In 1952 McLin achieved his goal of formally leading a hospital. He left Methodist to become the top administrator at Mound Park Hospital in St. Petersburg, Florida.

Mound Park was excellent experience for Community Hospital. McLin learned the complexities of leading a rapidly expanding hospital with an influential role in the community. A critical part of Mound Park's expansion was a strategic insight of McLin's: he saw that the superintendent's relationships with physicians were integral to the financial success of a hospital. The stronger the link between doctors and the hospital's formal leader, the more effective the organization was with patients and their families.

McLin also witnessed the unusual effects that hospital expansion could sometimes produce. The British spy novelist Ian Fleming had highlighted the hospital in his newest book, Live and Let Die. Mound Park was a widely visible organization in Florida and the southeastern United States. By extension, it meant that the formal leader of such a hospital needed to be creative, imaginative, and adaptable.

McLin's first actions as the new superintendent of Community Hospital showed his leadership skill. He recruited one of his team members at Mound Park to come north with him. William Newman was an administrative assistant who specialized in purchasing. McLin succeeded in convincing Newman to join the new executive team at Community Hospital. McLin wanted strong leadership in economic issues to build success at Community.

McLin built the rest of his team from there. Keeping the board of directors informed, McLin identified and hired Alys Kline, director of nursing, who immediately launched a hectic campaign to recruit nurses; Richard Condelaro, comptroller; Dr. Jack Mershon, laboratory; Dr. Clifford Taylor, X-Ray; Kenneth Gillmore, pharmacy;

Peggy Thomas, dietician; Marion Rigney, housekeeping; Herman Schnep, chief engineer and soon-to-be president of the Indiana Hospital Engineers Association; and Marilyn Behrandt, medical records. Other members were Angelo Bommisuto, kitchen manager; Mary McCaslin, personnel director; Virginia Bolen, central supply; Margaret Fulp, chief registrar; Edna Brackman, assistant comptroller; Lois Schultz, public relations; Dr. Samuel Doughty, Jr, chief anesthesiologist; and Gordon Boughton, administrative resident. This core group signaled an excellent start for McLin.

Condelaro, the comptroller, was a unique member of McLin's team. He had worked as an administrator for the past four years a few blocks away, at Norways Hospital Foundation, a private psychiatric facility. His place of birth, however, was hundreds of miles west in South Dakota. He was a Native American, belonging to the Oglala band of the Sioux tribe; his grandparents had lived during the era of Sitting Bull and Crazy Horse. Condelaro was a military veteran of both World War II and the Korean War, one of a small yet remarkable group of Native Americans to serve in both wars. He held two master's degrees and was a talented artist. He kept in contact with prominent Native American painters on the Great Plains. Condelaro's diverse background enriched the leadership at Community.

With the internal team in place, McLin began a long-term external relationship with the Irvington Union of Clubs, one of the groups so important to the founding of Community Hospital. McLin spoke to the Union's large membership about the nature of community life on the eastside of Indianapolis. He explained his vision for the part that Community Hospital would play in enriching the quality of life in Irvington and other neighborhoods in the eastern section of Marion County.

One of McLin's most important acts in the early operation of Community Hospital was to act on his insight from Mound Park. He seized upon the existing momentum of physician involvement in launching Community Hospital. By the time Emma Nicoll and other patients began to arrive at Community Hospital, McLin had recruited more than 400 doctors into a quasi-network of physicians. It was an astounding feat.

Besides McLin, Alma Bruck was another key leader vital to

the early operational success of Community Hospital. Newspaper reporters noted that the abundance of physicians active at Community Hospital was not matched by nurses. Barely any nurses had been hired by late 1956. Alma Bruck—board member and civic leader in both Irvington and Indianapolis—jumped into action.

Bruck was an imposing figure. Vocal, strong, and self-confident, Bruck was sixty-six years-old when Community Hospital opened. She prided herself on always being impeccably dressed and had a general disdain for what she described as "excessive informalities." She had three children with her husband, Louis, a well-known engineer in Indianapolis. Their eldest son had been killed in France during World War II and buried at Arlington National Cemetery. It was a loss she never forgot and one of her animating memories in forging attitudes about health care and families.

Bruck's leadership was exhaustive. She was a long-time member of the school board of Indianapolis's schools, having risen to the position of vice president. She never hestitated to tackle controversial issues in education, ranging from curriculum to student integration. She was also a lay leader at Irvington Presbyterian Church, an influential political activist in the Republican Party, and cultivated serious musical, artistic, and literary development in Indianapolis. Bruck molded the world in which she lived.

Bruck had accompanied McLin when he gave his formal speech to the Irvington Union of Clubs, a group which she led. Bruck had also given a speech that day on the importance of the new hospital and her vision of an innovative and dynamic bond between the organization and the community. This speech equalled McLin's as a vision of Community Hospital for eastern Indianapolis. Bruck explained the trust that people would place in the hospital, a trust that acted like water in a well, giving life and sustenance to those who drew from the depths.

Bruck also believed that women represented a vital resource for Community Hospital. She asserted, "Service is women's area," and that women needed their own organization if both they and the hospital were to realize the maximum power from their involvement.

At Downey Avenue Christian Church, Bruck guided the formation of the new Women's Auxiliary, of which she was elected president. Along with Bruck, more than 200 original members voted Mrs. E.W. Lollis as vice president of membership; Mrs. Charles D. Vawter vice president of volunteer services; Mrs. George W. Shaffer vice president of finance; Mrs. Francis Insley vice president of press relations; Mrs. Roy Geider corresponding secretary; Mrs. William Dyer assistant corresponding secretary; Mrs. D.M Kernahan recording secretary; Mrs J. Perry Meek, assistant recording secretary; Mrs Francis E. Dobbs treasurer; and Mrs. G.F. Romy assistant treasurer.

The group expected their work to include a gift shop, sewing, a "Stork Club" for new mothers, clerical duties, hosting in the hospital lobby, and when needed, providing housing in emergency situations. They decided on their own uniforms of "Cheery Cherry Red."

Bruck told the women that they would set the tone for the hospital. She also urged them to be visionary and inclusive, seeking out participants from throughout Marion County and not only in Irvington and eastern Indianapolis. She further announced that the Women's Auxiliary had received its first major donation, an award of $1000 as seed capital from the Irvington Union of Clubs, the organization she also led.

The shortage of nurses in 1956 captivated Bruck's attention. Under her leadership, the Women's Auxiliary rushed into action. They provided skilled volunteers who knew the practical applications of nursing. They filled slots in the schedules and helped care for Nicoll and other patients. Not surprisingly, an Indianapolis newspaper stated that the founding of the Women's Auxiliary was one of the most significant community events of the year.

Nursing vice president Alys Kline found and hired twenty nurses who, with volunteers from the Women's Auxiliary, managed to care for almost 100 patients on the fourth floor. At the same time the hospital's emergency room was overwhelmed with people who needed immediate care of minor conditions. Without more staff, Community Hospital turned away patients. 250 beds and 72 bassinets stood empty.

Board members Robert Efroymson, Alma Bruck, Willis Conner Jr, Luther Shirley, Fred Shick, Joseph Guidone, William Dyer Jr, John Siegesmund, Dr. James Denny, Dr. Floyd Boyer, and Dr. J.W. Wright

Sr contacted the Indianapolis Hospital Development Association and acquired an additional $250,000 to cover the expenses. The money helped Community Hospital continue to gather the needed workforce.

The excitement of funding and founding of the early and mid-1950s had shifted to the bumps and bruises of opening and implementation by the late 1950s. Within that time, however, Community Hospital had forged a spirit of family within the people who worked there and the patients who were treated there. A culture was forming.

Over the next several weeks and months, McLin, Kline, and the rest of the leadership team were tireless in filling full-time positions in nursing, labs, and support services. The hospital introduced a babysitting service operated by the Women's Auxiliary. By bringing their infants and young children to work under supervision, women were able to accept offers as nurses.

Kline's vibrant personality was an important factor in attracting nurses and nursing staff to Community. Quickly known in the hospital for her pink-toned office, Kline was enthusiastic, energetic, and devoted to the new hospital. Within months she had pulled together a department of more than 300 people, including nurses, aides, attendants, clerks, and technicians. Kline had served as Army Air Corp flight nurse over the Atlantic Ocean during World War II and after the war had helped open a new hospital in Savannah, Georgia before joining McLin's team. Those experiences gave Kline an invaluable maturity and steadiness that met the challenge of those early months at Community.

The work of Community Hospital's leaders and staff performed a near-miracle over the first year of operation. By 1957, Community Hospital's array of physicians had grown to 540 doctors, an increase of more than twenty percent. 11,500 people had used the hospital's services; more than 5000 surgeries were performed in six surgical units. Instead of the national average of two employees for every patient, Community Hospital had actually provided more pediatric, obstetric, surgical, and general medical care with an average of only 1.7 staff per patient.

Something else emerged. The struggle to both treat patients and at the same time find employees produced a "we're-in-this-together" attitude throughout Community Hospital. Many employees, such as Alys Kline, had seen this attitude during World War II. Kline encouraged her nursing staff to crystallize the spirit in a formal way. Kline and the registered nurses organized their own organization, the "Community Caps," while she assisted the licensed practical nurses to form their own group, the "Communiteers." In both cases, these bands of hospital co-workers and caregivers hosted dances, dinners, picnics, and teas for employees and their families. A similar spirit was reinforced by the Women's Auxiliary when it began to sponsor Christmas decorations and events for patients and staff alike. An observer judged the effect from these efforts was to create "the family atmosphere prevalent among employees of Community."

The family feeling deepened from a second source. The vast majority of the more than five hundred doctors linked to Community Hospital were family physicians. Dr. Floyd Boyer was one of the founding physicians and was the first medical chief of staff. He had had a family practice on the east side of Indianapolis since the 1930s. Boyer was held in high esteem throughout Indianapolis.

Robert Arnold was another example of a physician-leader at Community. Arnold had graduated from Indiana University School of Medicine in 1947. In deciding where to practice medicine as a family physician, Arnold had looked at a map of doctors' offices in the area and saw that few existed in eastern Marion County. He had built up an extensive practice among families in the vicinity of Irvington and when Community Hospital opened, he gladly led his patients there.

As a family physician, Arnold cared for parents and children in the same household. He was one of the most visible figures of authority and expertise to these families; they relied on him for advice and guidance in all things medical and came to regard him as an extension of themselves. Arnold expected that each of these families would receive the type of care from Community's staff that they would give to their own families; in many cases, it was literally true, they were caring for their own families. He, in turn, offered the same sort of relations to the staff, to his colleagues in other family practices, and to their patients as well. These attitudes interlocked invisibly as one after another, dozens by the dozens, Robert Arnold and these family doctors visited with patients in their rooms at Community Hospital, encouraged nurses and staff to handle them with the utmost care and respect, and reinforced the hospital's work with a professionalism and career identity all their own. "The people on the east side," Arnold said, "felt that this was their hospital."

Drs. Albert Blake, George Parker, and J.B. White were also part of the founding group of Community physicians. The hospital's location was a vital fact. Parker said, "This was my part of town and these were my patients." Blake noted that there were only generalists among the physicians; no sub-specialties existed. The doctors were family doctors, treating and knowing and caring for whole families who lived and worked near the new facility. White commented, "This was probably one of the finest groups of physicians in the city."

Many of the physicians lived within short distances of one another. They were tight-knit. McLin recognized the group's cohesion and pondered how he might encourage their mutual bond within the new hospital. Coffee was his answer. McLin had the kitchen staff brew fresh pots of coffee for use by the doctors. The doctors arrived early every day to Community, poured hot coffee in their favorite cup, and began to debate and consult with each other on patients and the latest medical journal or conference. The atmosphere was "incredible," a doctor said. McLin's self-styled physician coffee pots were the first of their kind in Indianapolis.

Coffee pots were one thing, board seats were quite another. Community's reliance on physician leadership went as deep as the hospital's articles of incorporation. The charter for Community stated that the medical staff would have the right to select doctors to fill one-fourth of the hospital's board of directors. That doctors held twenty-five percent of the board's seats was almost unheard-of in other healthcare organizations. Doctors occupied an important place at Community.

Almost immediately, doctors concluded that a special culture was blossoming. This was an extraordinary achievement, a powerful mark of Community Hospital's success in rapidly becoming an organization with an identity of itself. Its best expression was by a doctor who wrote an anonymous letter to a local newspaper in the late 1950s.

The doctor began, "We—you and I and many thousand others in the Indianapolis area—have built a new hospital. The architects that designed the Community Hospial did not follow precedent; they planned something different. The contractors and everybody concerned created something fresh and different."

The result, the doctor continued, is that "the existing atmosphere there is different. Through the hospital there are small signs 'donated by...' an organization, a group, an individual. Clearly, here, no one person or outfit has the edge—it is a community project accomplished. As a physician, I see one outstanding characteristic: the patient comes first... The patient has to come first."

The physician credited hospital leadership. McLin "has sacrificed no propriety, at the same time expediting needed action for the good of the patient." Kline and the nursing staff "has conquered the strangeness of new quarters, new acquaintances, and some brand new concepts that put them back into medicine."

The writer urged people at Community Hospital to understand the broad implications of what they had done and, more importantly, what they were now doing. "The Old World way," the doctor noted, "was in medicine best exemplified by the British patient system, for the patient to go to an institution, take what is given, and not wonder at continued symptoms." Community Hospital was carving a new path: "here in Indianapolis, the best way, the most human way, the American way, is established."

The doctor circled back to his point earlier in the letter: patients first. "The pharmacist chases over the city to find the one particular drug needed—not the near substitute; the dietician finds a troublesome way of preparing a feeding for one particular needing patient; the central supply sends material up to the room before the doctor takes his coat off; and so it has gone from top to bottom and all around; a helpful and willing smile is the badge of membership."

"As a physician," the writer concluded, "I wanted to congratulate the people of this area for a recapturing of all the best. We openly are 'involved in mankind,' together, successfully. This is our Hospital."

A remarkable statement.

With such a culture in place, Community Hospital enjoyed

a substantial period of success through the end of the 1950s. The hospital became the site of a full-time ambulance crew, transporting an abundance of patients to the facility from southeastern Marion County. The surrounding neighborhoods and the Shadeland Avenue business corridor became interwoven with Community Hospital. A new bus line conveyed many workers to and from the hospital.

Employers ranging from mammoth Western Electric to such small companies as the Allis-Chalmers dealership sent injured workers to the hospital; "it was our hospital," said P.E. MacAllister later, as he thought back to this period. MacAllister's father had owned the dealership. The rapidly growing area also featured legions of expectant mothers. Joining with the Indianapolis chapter of the American Red Cross, Community's doctors and nurses organized classes for first-time mothers. The Maternity-Family League started parenting and family classes, while the Marion County Heart Committee convened weight control sessions at the hospital.

The Women's Auxiliary emerged as a powerful bridge between the hospital and the community. Membership in Bruck's organization exploded ten-fold to 2800 women belonged to the group by the end of the 1950s. 500 members received awards at a ceremony in 1958. Through "card parties" and other fundraising activities, they continued to gather financial support for Community, including the opening of a physical therapy department. They sewed 20,000 garments annually, made draperies for each patient room, and performed all the landscaping duties. They raised more money for the hospital through "card parties." They continued to supplement nursing care, working in groups of ten with selected floors. They gained public recognition by working with 500 Boy Scouts on Paul Bunyan Day to install a 20-year beautification plan. Some members of the Women's Auxiliary took on additional part-time jobs and donated their earnings to Community. Bruck's group was a dynamic force.

An array of donations arrived at Community. Gifted money from Chi Omega Society purchased an electro-cardiograph machine. Teenagers from Thomas Howe High School—a school which Bruck had helped create—donated a specialized scales for babies. In nearby Hancock County a car dealership gave a station wagon for Community to use as a staff car. The Irvington Women's Lions Club paid for an Interfaith Quiet Room. With all this activity, board member Willis Conner Jr asserted in November 1959 that Community Hospital had established a "pattern of success" that other healthcare facilities could follow.

Community Hospital remained at high levels of activity in recruiting staff. Alys Kline designed a forty-hour training program for women interested in serving as volunteer nurses-aides. They would take temperatures, pulses, and respiration as well as conduct selected pre- and post-operative care. Another program targeted students from Arsenal Technical High School who worked fifteen hours a week at the hospital and studied one hour per week in health-related curriculum. Students completing the program acquired jobs as practical nurses and lab technicians at Community. Warren Central High School introduced a Future Nurses Club with 104 members and planned for a special chapter at Community Hospital.

The capstone in Community's workforce development was a unique partnership with Indiana Central University (now the University of Indianapolis). Community's nursing staff worked closely with the university's faculty to crystallize the first four-year college program for nurses in Indiana. The program featured the re-design of a university dorm into the center of the nursing program. Students went to Community Hospital for on-site lessons and experience.

By 1959 Community Hospital had arrived at its first crucial point. Robert Efroymson, chair of the hospital board, stepped down. He had been among the first since the early 1950s to conceive of building Community Hospital. Now, he stood aside for his successor, Fred Shick, a vice president at Indiana National Bank, to take his place at the head of the Community Hospital conference table.

Within weeks, Shick and McLin were in discussions of a creative strategic enterprise between Community Hospital and Sertoma Foundation. They envisioned the construction of a facility for elderly people on part of the property given by Edward Gallahue.

With a growing family spirit and a willingness to take risks, the people of Community Hospital looked into a new decade and saw change and opportunity in a bright future.

CHAPTER 4

Changing Fast, 1960-1969

The decade that dawned in 1960 was a time of rapid change for Community Hospital. Though hindsight suggested the change in these years was steady and sure, the actual experience at Community Hospital involved speed, adaptability, and fast-moving decisions. With more than 51,000 patients treated and 10,000 babies born by 1960 and 300 babies born monthly by 1962, Community Hospital's historic founding matured into broader organizational success.

For Community Hospital, the beginning of the 1960s included two of the most exciting changes in the organization's history.

The first was in September 1960. Community Hospital's success in attracting patients and deepening relations with residents and employers in the area produced an unanticipated problem: money flooded in from grateful patients and their families as well as from important organizations in eastern Marion County. It presented the happy dilemma of how to responsibly handle the incoming funds so as to honor the wishes of donors and, in so doing, encourage future donors to make contributions to the hospital.

For months discussions had been under way among McLin and the hospital's board members about "the need to establish a group to regulate and safekeep donations received by the hospital." The solution emerged by late 1960. McLin and board chair Fred Shick announced the formation of a Community Hospital Foundation. The foundation's design, McLin and Shick asserted, was specific and strategic. They determined that the Foundation would not raise money directly; the purpose was to receive money that the hospital's patrons had urged the hospital to accept. Moreover, the Foundation would not spend any money on hospital operations or expansion. No physical space and no tangible material would be the object of expenditure. Instead, the Foundation would concentrate its resources on research in two fields—the quality of care and the cost of care. The Foundation's mission was to ensue the continuous elevation of the former while relentlessly decreasing the latter.

McLin and Shick weren't done. They further stated that the Foundation would have its own board of directors. Members of the new board would function as hospital "ambassadors" who shared good news about the organization throughout Indianapolis, Marion County, and central Indiana. Intriguingly, board members would have a secondary duty as well: they would act as advisors to any committees which Community's own board of directors decided to establish.

In an important sense, this dual responsibility of the Foundation's board reflected the continued powerful impact of Alma Bruck. She had been adamant in exploring new ways for Community Hospital and its surrounding neighborhoods to interact and intersect with each other. Not satisifed with ordinary habits of occasional donations and volunteering, Bruck had prodded people to develop additional methods for involvement and support. McLin and Shick's vision of dualistic roles by Foundation board members was an attempt to intensify the connections between Community Hospital and the people who cherished it.

Finally, McLin and Shick, along with the hospital board, knew that the right leader had to be picked for the Foundation's board. Without an effective leader, the hospital's newest strategic initiative might drift into oblivion. They found their leader.

He was Edward B. Newell. Newell had just retired as vice president and general manager of the Allison Division of General Motors. Both Allison and General Motors had been major contributors to the original fundraising drive of 1952-1955. Newell was part of that effort. He was also familiar with creative projects and risk-oriented enterprises, having overseen Allison's experimentation with jet-engine propulsions and aircraft test flights designed for potential space travel and high-altitude bombing and surveillance.

A talented board of directors served with Newell. They were Jack Killen, Reily Adams, C. Harvey Bradley, Mrs. Alma Bruck, John Collett, Dr. James Denny, William Dyer Jr, Dr. I. Lynn Esch, James Gloin, Joseph Guidone, G. Barron Mallory, George Oliver Sr, and Luther Shirley. A large share of these members were veterans of the hospital board. They acted as institutional memory of the hospital's roots as well as creative and engaging thinkers and problem-solvers. Newell and the board gave the Foundation a solid start.

Community Hospital made more history with a second major change in the early 1960s. In January 1961 McLin announced the opening of Indianapolis's first "intensive care unit" in a private hospital. The ICU featured experienced registered nurses who provided 24-hour care to patients in the units. Each nurse had responsibility for two patients. These patients had critical needs: heart cases requiring oxygen, victims of severe burns and trauma, and brain-related operations. The fifteen patient rooms that comprised the ICU were arranged in a half-circle with three of the beds reserved for emergency uses.

McLin saw the ICU as a test case for Community Hospital's expansion in the near-term future. He used the ICU project to help his executive team and indeed the entire hospital better understand how to launch a new program or a new initiative. Among the most active participants in the ICU project were Drs. Charles Cure, R.B. Rust, Richard Worley, Ted Grisell, John Thompson, David Lozow, and Charles Knowles. Utilizing timelines, projected resources, anticipated staffing, and built-in strategic goals, the ICU project enabled the doctors, nurses, and support personnel to sharpen their ability at envisioning and achieving a far-reaching goal. The ICU was, McLin stated, "a pilot" for growth that the hospital could employ again in future expansions.

The new ICU showed that Community Hospital was intent upon innovation in the new decade. McLin, Kline, and several of Community's doctors had closely followed an emerging national trend in healthcare, the deployment of semi-circular space designs. This form of spatial organization improved patient care by reducing the distance nurses had to walk to address patient needs. The ICU reminded everyone that the spirit of positive change which had sprouted in Marion County's eastern soil was still producing excellence in healthcare.

Within six months, the ICU project opened the door for an even bolder expansion. By late 1961 McLin declared that Community Hospital was building a new wing onto the original structure. The expansion added more than 200 beds to the hospital's capacity. A rehabilitation facility and a diagnostics and treatment center were contained within the new expansion.

The boldness was in the design. Enlarging the ICU semi-circular model into an entire multi-floor space, McLin unveiled the "Twin Towers" design of fully circular levels for patients. "The arrangement," said new board chair Charles Baker, a prominent Indianapolis attorney, "enables a nurse to observe all beds from her central position and saves her many steps." The fundamental purpose of the expansion was improvement of patient care through quicker and easier nursing access. The vision of the Twin Towers rested on multiplying the advantages of the ICU into the total design of two entire buildings.

The Twin Towers became one of the defining leadership moments of Community Hospital. The cost of the facility—$4 million, half of the cost to build Community Hospital almost ten years before— presented a financial challenge. McLin and the board of directors disagreed over the strategy to pay for expansion. One group, led by former fundraising leader and board member Willis Conner, Jr, argued for repeating the pioneering effort of raising money from local residents, businesses, and organizations. Here was the chance, Conner asserted, for Community Hospital to deepen its founding imprint. Another group, which included McLin and incoming board chairman Charles Baker, doubted the ability of the region to raise the money privately again. Baker and his colleagues reflected some of the hints of doubt contained in Richard Nixon's speech at the groundbreaking ceremony seven years earlier. They urged the use of government funds, especially those from the federal government.

Both groups sought to protect their view of the founding "community" philosophy of Community Hospital. For Conner and his colleagues, much of Community Hospital's identity was rooted in the economic story of its founding. They viewed the opening up of pocketbooks and company bank accounts as powerful expressions of community support. McLin, Baker, and others embraced this view, too, but they also believed it existed in the feeling of "family" that bound together doctors, nurses, patients, and neighbors of Community Hospital. They regarded governmental funding as secondary to the emerging cultural identity of the people working for or served by the hospital.

Within the walls of the C. Harvey Bradley Board room, the discussions consumed several weeks of debate, heated and intense. Finally, the board voted unanimously in November 1961 to seek $1.6 million in federal funds. Within a year, through the intercession of Hoosier Democratic officials in Washington DC, Community Hospital obtained another $1 million from the federal Department of Health, Education, and Welfare.

The board's handling of this deeply emotional debate was crucial to its outcome. Both groups were passionate in their opinions. Both groups were confident that their outlooks pointed toward successful futures. Both groups understood that they were at a key juncture in the hospital's existence. People from both groups argued, disagreed, and debated.

Such a clash wasn't surprising. The board was comprised of influential people with respected records of service in businesses, community organizations, and more. The essential point was that rather than slide into rancor and division, the board turned the issue in a positive direction. Baker and Conner agreed that the decision on funding required a unanimous vote of support by board members. Whichever group garnered a greater number of board votes, the other group would have to agree to alter their final vote to produce a united decision. This was a historic move that was not mandated or preordained. The board determined that unity and cohesion were invaluable principles and its members acted on that belief.

The Community board's cohesion was all the more impressive

in light of influential public opposition. Three members of the Indianapolis Hospital Development Association's board resigned in protest against Community's decision. In addition, the Indianapolis News editorial staff published a scathing account of Community board's vote, applauding the three resignations. Despite this public pressure in mid-summer 1962, Community Hospital stood firm in its decision.

This was a moment of extraordinary importance. A sizeable portion of the entity that helped oversee Community's founding—the Indianapolis Hospital Development Association—had attacked the decision of the hospital to accept governmental funds. Local media had endorsed the attack. And yet, the Community board stayed united as a bulwark of the hospital's purpose, the hospital's principles and values, the hospital's founding as an expression of community in its most basic and fundamental form. Perhaps more than anything else, here was a choice that refounded the founding.

A ceremony at 6pm ceremony on Wednesday, February 20, 1963 highlighted the launch of the Twin Towers' construction. A team from Community Hospital organized the event. They arranged for loudspeakers to broadcast a telephone call to the first babies born at Community Hospital, Brian and Bruce Gray (delivered on October 16, 1956). Now six years old, the two young boys phoned into the ceremony from their home in Arizona. The physician who delivered the two boys, Dr. Frederick Rice, stood holding the phone with a large group outside Community Hospital. The phone rang, the boys could be heard asking for the digging to begin, and Dr. Rice pushed his shovel into the ground. The crowd cheered. Later that evening, the group met for a special banquet.

Like the first building at Community Hospital, the construction of the Twin Towers included the formation of a time capsule. The capsule was another metal box with photos, brochures, and other contents. One difference between the Twin Towers and the original building was that patients in their existing rooms stared out their windows at the new construction. This wasn't a new organization growing out of the ground; it was an existing organization evolving into a new form. The patients watched the completion of the Twin Towers and talked with nurses and doctors alike about the daily progress on the new facility. Progress stalled when an Indianapolis labor strike pulled plumbers off the building project for a time in autumn 1963.

Another delay with a tragic human cost occurred that autumn. On October 31, 1963, at the Indiana State Fair Coliseum roughly five miles from Community Hospital, containers with oxygen and other gasses exploded during an ice-skating show. The blast hurled large chunks of concrete through the air. People were tossed more than fifty feet by the force of the explosion. Seventy-four people died. Another four hundred were injured.

Community Hospital received seventy-five patients from the tragedy that night. Among them were several pregnant women who went into labor because of stress from the disaster. They were taken to the obstetrics department at Community Hospital; Drs. Robert Arnold, Don Cline, and others delivered more than a dozen infants during the next few hours. In addition, others doctors at the hospital jumped in their cars and raced to nearby hospitals to assist in emergency treatments. Not until the end of 1963 was the last patient from the accident released from Community Hospital. The hospital's doctors, nurses, and staff had collaborated with other hospitals in Indianapolis to help local residents cope with and recover from the day's tragic events.

Death visited Community Hospital again, this time in July 1964, claiming the life of one of the key overseers of the Twin Towers project. Richard Condelaro had been tasked with ensuring a smooth building project. On July 3, seated at his office desk, Condelaro suffered a massive heart attack. He died just minutes later. The loss was staggering to the tight-knit family of Community staff. Alma Bruck would express the grief everyone felt at the hospital—she started a campaign to raise money for a scholarship in Condelaro's honor and to contract with an artist to paint his portrait, a fitting honor for the talented Sioux native. Bruck would search throughout Condelaro's home state of South Dakota for an authentic wooden frame made from a pioneer barn. Anything less than true frontier material would dishonor him, Bruck said, for "there was nothing false or feigned about Dick Condelaro."

A few months later, on October 31, 1964, the people of Community Hospital assembled for a happier occasion. A formal ceremony celebrated the opening of the Twin Towers.

The Twin Towers were among the most remarkable medical buildings in the Midwest. Designed by architect James Lewis, the Twin Towers were the only radial-design healthcare structures in Indiana and one of only three in the United States. They featured the latest technological offerings, such as in-room monitors for the patient's pulse, temperature, respiration, electro-cardiagram, and encephalogram. Oxygen was pumped directly to the bed. A nursing station stood no more than ten feet away from every patient room. The Twin Towers also contained x-ray facilities, outpatient and short-term treatment space, rehabilitation capacities, and a speech and hearing clinic.

Nurse Cleo Burgard, who went on to become a key hospital leader in quality and risk management, was among those who opened the Towers for patients. At first, Burgard and the other nurses—each of whom were clad in white uniforms—were confused and uncertain about the circular design of the patient units. She helped her team of nurses develop procedures and routines that shortened the time between a patient's call for assistance and a nurse's response. Burgard demonstrated a passion for details and follow-up, two qualities that would make her one of Community's most outstanding nurses.

Community Hospital's chairman of the board of trustees, George Kuhn, declared at the Twin Tower ceremony that the building embodied the hospital's commitment to "good patient care...everything else," he said, "comes after that." The keynote speaker, Federal Judge William Steckler, used the occasion to frame a new trend in healthcare: the use of emergency rooms as a family's on-demand medical center. Steckler pointed out that usage of Community Hospital's emergency facilities had risen almost 400% in less than a decade. Steckler noted that the high degree of individual mobility would only intensify the trend. Buried in his prediction was his assumption that the local economy would remain prosperous, adding to the mobility. Steckler asserted that Community Hospital should pioneer a reformation of practice in emergency medicine, seeking to strike a balance between the interests of doctors, patients, and hospitals. Steckler's speech challenged Community Hospital to stay and thrive in the forefront of healthcare, producing changes rather than reacting to them.

The Steckler challenge coincided with the introduction of several changes at Community Hospital to improve patient care. Waiting hours for families and friends were reduced to help conserve the energy of patients and, it was hoped, shorten their recovery time. Patient room rates rose by a dollar, while a campaign began—Tamba the cartoon elephant was the visual image of the program—to draw attention to new safety procedures. Meanwhile, a shortage of qualified nurses continued to worry hospital officials. The issue had reached a crisis point in the minds of McLin and his executive team. They broadened recruiting efforts to nursing programs at more than twenty colleges and universities in addition to its marque program at Indiana Central College (the University of Indianapolis).

Steckler's challenge also reached beyond patient care. A nationally renowed fundraising expert came to Community Hospital to discuss new ways to raise money from surrounding businesses and organizations. The effort reflected among Community Hospital's leaders to continue to enhance the local spirit of private and community-based financing of the organization.

At the midway point in the 1960s, Community Hospital and its Twin Towers stood tall in greater Indianapolis. The Women's Auxiliary and its new president, Mrs. Francis Insley, hit upon the idea of using the impressive structures as a Christmas beacon for the east side of Marion County. They purchased a blue-lighted Christmas tree and placed it atop the Twin Towers. Neighbors for miles around Community Hospital began a decades-long tradition of marking part of the Christmas season with the sight of the tree shining a brilliant blue from the hospital's rooftop, one of the highest points in eastern Indianapolis.

The Women's Auxiliary maintained its value as one of the strongest links between Community Hospital and the surrounding neighborhoods. The group gathered more than a hundred volunteers for "candy-stripe" service and helped develop the idea of wrapping new-born babies in Christmas stockings for their mothers; future employee Donna Curran was born at Community and came home in one of these stockings. In 1965 the Auxiliary also began a "first" in local fundraising with a unique program at the popular Wasson's Department Store in the new Eastgate Shopping Center, a focal point of economic development near the bustling and heavily industrialized Shadeland Avenue. Auxiliary volunteers worked for a day at the store in Eastgate Shopping Center in an effort to highlight National Hospital Week. Proceeds from Wasson's on that day went to Community Hospital for new equipment purchases. Clinical employees from Community Hospital also demonstrated mock surgical procedures at Eastgate. Other organizations in central Indiana closely watched these events for replication in their fundraising.

In 1965 a tidal wave of change crashed into Community Hospital and the rest of American healthcare—Medicare and Medicaid. President Lyndon Johnson signed into law the programs that reshaped medicine and medical treatment across the United States. Medicare provided hospital and medical insurance to people over age 65, numbering 19 million Americans. Medicaid offered medical insurance to recipients of direct cash assistance. Payroll taxes helped pay for the programs. A new age of federal government involvement and intervention in healthcare had arrived.

Judged by the program's requirements, the effect of Medicare and Medicaid on Community Hospital appeared small. The elderly and poor combined did not comprise the majority of Community Hospital's patients. But that fact didn't measure the full story of the law's powerful impact.

The law had a significance for Community Hospital unlike other healthcare facilities. US President Lyndon Johnson envisioned the programs as fulfillment of former President Harry Truman's attempt to implement national medical insurance in the late 1940s; both men were Democrats. Truman was a guest at Johnson's official signing of the law as well as the first recipient of a Medicare card. Truman was an arch foe and vocal opponent of Eisenhower and Nixon, each of whom had played public roles in the founding of Community Hospital. In addition, Johnson attached the programs to the Social Security Act of 1935, the cornerstone of President Franklin Roosevelt's New Deal, which was the philosophical opposite of Eisenhower and Nixon's anti-New Deal endorsement of the Community Hospital project.

Medicare and Medicaid also had a substantial practical impact on Community Hospital. Medicare and Medicaid inserted a new element—the federal government—into the work of Community Hospital's doctors, nurses, and staff. The federal government became a major force in determining fees and prices for services as well as selecting how and which services would qualify for governmental payments. Hospital employees had to learn the best ways to advise patients and families to enroll in the programs. Both Medicare and Medicaid hired staff of their own to administer the programs and in so doing expanded the scope of personnel interacting with Community Hospital employees.

The response of Community Hospital to these major changes reflected the quality of its people. Newly re-titled by Community Hospital's board of trustees as the hospital's President, Wilbur McLin was selected by the Indiana Hospital Association to lead a statewide committee that planned new policies for implementing Medicare and Medicaid. McLin's efforts on the committee helped the hospital stay abreast of important adjustments in the two programs. McLin also belonged to the Hospital Research Development Institute (HRDI), a 25-person initiative that brought together important hospital leaders to consider new innovations.

Leadership is about more than holding official titles. As important as McLin's work in governmental programs and HRDI was, Community Hospital's adaptation to the programs further reflected the leadership of doctors and healthcare professionals throughout the organization. And in that spirit of leadership, Community Hospital not only adapted to the new era, it blossomed.

Beginning in 1966 Community Hospital introduced a series of trailblazing innovations. Five doctors—Drs. Edwin Eaton, Rolla Burghard, Charles Seaman, K. Douglas Marshall, and Howard Williams—formed a corporation to provide comprehensive medical coverage of the emergency room and to streamline treatment of cases according to severity. This was one of the first examples in the nation of a permanent group of emergency-room physicians based in a hospital.

In addition, Community Hospital opened its first cardiac care unit. Conceived by Drs. Berj Antreasian and Charles Wunsch, the new unit consisted of four beds, specially trained nurses (led by Mary Ann Brown), and portable cardiac monitors and emergency resuscitation equipment. The cardiac care unit began at nearly the same time as the emergency room corporation, generating an atmosphere of creativity, risk-taking, and boldness. Within three years, a cardiac catherization laboratory began and the cardiac care unit was the largest in Indianapolis. Both Antreasian and Wunsch gained prominence as two of the most important physician-leaders at the hospital

More innovations were unveiled at Community Hospital. The Women's Auxiliary raised money to purchase a photo coagulator for damaged retinas, one of the first models of this type in Indiana. The hospital's first chaplain, Reverend William Hogsett, joined the staff, as did Robert Reilly, newly hired chief of security. Community Hospital stepped forward as the first medical client of a new company in Indianapolis; United Hospital Services began to offer a variety of services to reduce expenses at hospitals. Community was the first to ship its laundry every day to the new facility. Capping it all was the announcement of a planned $3.9 million expansion for 150 more beds, nurseries, medical records facility, medical libraries, and chapel.

As the close of 1966 approached, a tenth-anniversary event was held at Community Hospital. The original board members of Community Hospital were honored at a dinner where they received citations and certificates of gratitude for their work. Edward Gallahue and Robert Efroymson, among others, praised the hospital for striving for new success and for its commitment to the community.

Gallahue, Efromyson, and the rest of the original board members at the ceremony recognized that their vision of a uniquely conceived Community Hospital had come to fruition. This result often took on unusual forms that reached beyond healthcare. That had proven true with the blue-light Christmas tree. It proved true again on April 4, 1968 when Indianapolis, like the American nation at large, stared into the face of severe crisis and chaos. Community Hospital was part of the story on that fateful night.

In the late afternoon of April 4, 1968 civil rights leader Martin Luther King Jr was shot by an assassin in Memphis, Tennessee. He died less than two hours later. Scarcely minutes after reports of King's death, riots began to erupt in major cities across the United States. Outraged city residents, many of them black, protested in the streets. Violence exploded with dozens injured, hundreds arrested, and extensive destruction of cars, stores, and other buildings. Intensifying tensions in cities since 1965, the American urban landscape seemed on the brink of total breakdown and social disorder. Interestingly, Indianapolis was the largest American city not to have a significant riot on the night of King's murder. The reason, commentators said at the time (and since), was a historic speech delivered by Democratic presidential candidate Robert Kennedy at a basketball court in Indianapolis. The crowd of roughly 1,000 people who heard Kennedy's speech dispersed nonviolently.

Kennedy's speech was truly remarkable and played a key role in calming tensions. However, other local residents did so as well and here was where Community Hospital was the scene of an intriguing story. A young, 23-year old nurse, Carol Olsen, was in charge of the night shift at Community Hospital. Tall and gangly, Olsen was white, had grown up in a relatively affluent and racially homogeneous suburb of Chicago, and had no experience or training in general supervision, let alone conflict resolution, crisis management, and racial diversity. Olsen's duties included supervising the night-shift maintenence crews, most of whom were black. By 11pm April 4, when Olsen's shift began, these employees were wracked with grief and seething with hostility. Olsen had to decide what to do. The hospital, like the rest of Indianapolis on the night of April 4, was a likely spot for confrontations and upheaval.

For a few minutes Olsen gathered her thoughts privately in her small office. She then opened her office door and went into the hall of one of the floors in the Twin Towers. She asked the employees to gather around her in the hall. Once there, listening yet angry, the night-shift maintenance employees heard Olsen speak about the tragedy of King's death, the purpose of his life, and the responsibility she and they shared together for their work on behalf of Community

Hospital's patients. She pointed to the hospital itself as their equal and common ground. She was nervous and unsure, but her sincerity and genuineness were evident. Olsen's impromptu remarks—never heard by anyone except these workers—calmed the tensions. The night passed peacefully at Community Hospital.

The next day, Wilbur McLin and Chaplain William Hogsett anticipated, regardless of Kennedy's speech, more employees could be upset by King's death. To help them cope with the tragedy, McLin and Hogsett organized a day-long observation of King's death and his legacy. McLin and Hogsett arranged schedules of employees to allow each unit and floor to have black and white staff, nurses, and doctors share their grief together. They prayed, watched television coverage of King's funeral from Morehouse College in Atlanta, Georgia, and whispered condolences to each other. "I wanted it brought to the public's attention," Community Hospital supervisor Maggie Posey wrote a few days later in a letter to the editor of the Indianapolis Star, "that if all hospital directors were such as ours, having all employees' best interests at heart, we as a (black) race would never need to march or die for a cause again."

It was a profound statement.

Peace endured in Indianapolis during those awful days because organizations like Community Hospital and its leaders contributed to an atmosphere of saddened respect and mutual suffering.

The strong bond among the employees of Community Hospital was tested by another tragedy only a few days after King's death. The ten-year old son of Thomas Wilburn, an assistant administrator under McLin and an aspiring leader with staggering potential, died at Community Hospital from pneumonia. Wilburn was a popular figure at the hospital and his son received a lot of attention from staff. Coming so soon after King's demise, the boy's death darkened the spirits of many doctors, nurses, and staff at Community Hospital.

Wilburn was determined to carry on with his administrative duties at Community. He plunged into his work and organized a special committee to improve efficiencies at the organization. The "Cost Reduction Committee" identified three people for special commendations in their quest to reduce waste and unnecessary expenses. Wilburn gave awards to Gladys Ramsey (hospital buyer), Richard Johnson (director of housekeeping), and Millard Jorgensen (manager of stores) for their diligence in saving money. The committee, in turn, praised Wilburn for his leadership and sacrifice in a time of intense personal loss. The bond at Community Hospital served as a web of support for employees at all levels of the organization.

The bond was also visible in quieter moments too. McLin's executive team and the hospital's unit managers decided to reach out to physically challenged residents of Indianapolis. Spearheaded by rehabilitation specialist Beverly Distelhorst, they acquired from the Indianapolis Chapter of the National Paraplegic Foundation a special chair that enabled an adult paraplegic to work independently at the hospital. Distelhorst's actions were instrumental in hiring paraplegic employees at Community Hospital.

The 1960s closed at Community Hospital on a rising tide. The discouragement of recent public and private tragedies gave way to a flow of better events. The Women's Auxiliary conducted one of its most ambitious fundraisers ever with the sponsorship of the musical "Oliver" at the local Eastwood Theater. A new volunteer program began; elderly husbands of members of the Women's Auxiliary formed into a "Redcoat" brigade. These Redcoated older men devoted specific hours each week to helping care for the housekeeping needs of patients, organizing medical records, and maintaining public relations materials in lobbies, waiting areas, and other local distributions.

Most of all, growth in patient care had exploded in recent months. With births continuing to expand, such doctors as Robert Arnold urged the adoption of the latest equipment to satisfy the demand. Dr. Arnold led the effort to purchase an "air-fluidized bed", the first ever secured by a private hospital. The bed improved patient comfort, enhanced the sterility of conditions surrounding the patient, and offered a wider range of use beyond obstetrics. The new equipment earned substantial media coverage for Community Hospital.

Community's expansion involved a new cardiovascular program. Dr. Jean Mercho, a recent arrival at Community, convinced both McLin and the board to approve development of the program in 1969. Mercho was meticulous in gathering the necessary data to launch the effort. The board was worried about costs; Mercho offered to buy the first heart pump. Impressed by Mercho's evidence, McLin and the board waved off the suggestion. They voted to forge ahead with the program. Mercho added Dr. Hussan Rousdi to his initiative.

Mercho and Rousdi's first patient was a twenty-one year-old woman suffereing from a heart rupture. They performed surgery on her over a six-hour period. Mercho stayed with her in her room while she recovered. Around nine in the morning, almost twelve hours later, she opened her eyes. Mercho was ecstatic. The cardiovascular program celebrated its first success.

The growth in obsterics and heart treatment extended to other parts of Community Hospital. The hospital had experienced more than 100% growth in emergency and outpatient usage in just over three years. Now, less than five years after opening the Twin Towers, McLin announced that work would commence on a $1.4 million expansion of the emergency department and outpatient clinic.

Community Hospital ended the 1960s riding a current of expansion and innovation. More doctors emerged with new ideas and new techniques for medical programs. The hospital adapted to change driven by both the surrounding neighborhoods—in the form of more social mobility and on-demand healthcare—and by the federal government—in the form of Medicare and Medicaid. The defining identity of dedicated doctors, nurses, and staff, which grew out of the founding soil of Ritter Avenue and eastern Marion County, had carried the hospital through a decade of tumult and upheaval. Few people suspected that this was only the preface to a bigger story.

CHAPTER 5
Of Layers and Levels, 1970-1972

Not all change is the same. Even the major changes, which at a distance may look alike, are more diverse and unique when seen at a closer vantage point. Community Hospital had undergone fundamental change with the rise of Medicare and Medicaid and the prevalence of on-demand medical treatments in an emergency department. But more, and different, changes were ahead in the 1970s and they included some of the most important challenges any organization, any hospital, could face. Change had layers and change had levels.

The decade began with uncertainty and some confusion. Within a span of a few months, Community Hospital lowered prices and then, in a reversal, raised them. The fluctuation in room rates reflected the influence of Medicare and Medicaid's governmental procedures and complications in keeping costs linked to revenue. In addition, the hospital's emergency room was dangerously small and outdated. Community President Wilbur McLin urged the Indianapolis police department not to send any more ambulances to the hospital. The emergency room was filled and no more emergency patients could be taken. Police officials had to divert ambulances to other hospitals in the city.

It was no wonder that in April 1970 more than 700 Women's Auxiliary members packed an auditorium in Community Hospital to hear Vice President Thomas Wilbert explain the plan to expand

and upgrade the facility. Wilbert showed how the completed building project would enhance Community's capacity to deal with emergency cases. The new capacity promised a cascading effect where other departments in the hospital would have more time for ordinary patients.

While work on the expansion project neared completion, Community Hospital continued to push hard for more innovations in local healthcare. The nation's foremost expert on aging and end-of-life care, Dr. Elizabeth Kubler-Ross, spent time with nurses and doctors from Community Hospital. She told them to emphasize the quality of life—not just the extension of life—as a basic concern for people facing death. Kubler-Ross recommended a review of how patients were actively involved with vital medical decisions after learning they would die.

Kubler-Ross's appearance was a form of ongoing medical education for Community Hospital personnel. The hospital deepened its commitment to more education later in 1970 with the hiring of its first medical education director, Dr. George Parker. Parker's task was to help doctors keep pace with medicine's fastest breaking changes. Parker would work closely with Community Hospital's director of education and training, Nate Aldrich, who had learning responsibilities for the rest of hospital personnel. It was Aldrich who, with McLin's support, had first sent employees like Wilma Peacock to a special educational program at Wittenberg University in Ohio.

The program inspired Peacock to become an internal leader at Community in the years to come. Peacock went on to create a visiting-animal program to calm and soothe patients at the hospital. She brought in a llama, myna bird, and chinchillas in partnership with the Indianapolis Zoo. She helped establish a credit program to offset costs for low-income patients. She and her colleagues built a relationship with local dentists to provide services to patients. The investment of McLin in the growth of Peacock and other Community employees repaid tenfold in benefits to the hospital, its patients, and the surrounding neighborhoods.

On November 13, 1970 the much-anticipated expansion was done. A ceremony not only marked the opening of the new emergency center and outpatient facility, but it honored a trio of people who had been key movers behind the expansion. George Kuhn, Walter Pagenkopf, and James Gloin received special honors for the expansion.

The new capacity for emergency medicine consisted of eighteen holding beds, seven diagnostic beds, an isolation room, a shock room, and waiting areas. The outpatient space included conference facilities for doctors, a central area for nurses, seven examination rooms, a pair of cast rooms, and additional waiting and supply square footage.

Five years earlier, in 1965, leaders of Community Hospital had talked about the rise of on-demand medicine and healthcare. Now, standing in a new decade with a substantial boost to its emergency and outpatient services, Community Hospital offered a greater capacity than ever to the people of eastern Indianapolis and Marion County.

These changes at Community Hospital were planned and projected. A bigger change, of a magnitude for which none were prepared, lay just ahead.

Six months after opening the newest parts of Community Hospital, Wilbur McLin conducted another scheduled meeting of the board of directors. It was a Monday evening, May 24, 1971, the standard time and day for gatherings of Community board members. McLin and the group enjoyed dinner, held a normal meeting with reports on operations and updates on key activities. Shortly before 9pm, McLin thanked the attendees, dismissed the meeting, and went to his office. Sitting down in his chair, McLin prepared to tidy up his desk before going back to his home at 5555 North Arlington Street.

He never got up from behind his desk again.

A flash of pain ripped across the inside of McLin's chest. His history of heart problems had reasserted itself. A heart attack ensued. McLin slumped forward. A doctor who was in the board room waiting for McLin, entered his office a few minutes later and tried to resuscitate him. McLin was dead.

He died in the same chair where Richard Condelaro had sat when he passed away.

The next day, a newspaper ran a front-page headline: "W.C. McLin, Hospital Board President, Dies."

The implications were clear. A news reporter described McLin as "widely regarded as one of the nation's top administrators in hospital expansion." Another stated that McLin "had the spark of competence" and "a busy man's ability to do a lot of things." McLin was noteworthy for "his contribution to the modernization of hospitals" and that he "led and invigorated wherever he moved." McLin's skill was growth, and he left an imprint on Community Hospital that kept the organization thinking constantly about how to grow its space, its reach, its impact on the lives of people and neighborhoods. A source of identity and leadership was now gone. A void opened up.

McLin's passing was part of an unusual triangle of death for Community Hospital in mid-1971. Just days before McLin's fatal heart attack, Willis Conner Jr, the man many regarded as the public face of Community's original fundraising drive in the early 1950s, had also died. And two months after McLin's demise, Edward Gallahue fell victim to a life-ending illness at age 69. Three months' time, three leaders dead, and the people of Community Hospital stared at an unknown future. The void had become a chasm.

The situation was fraught with peril. The deaths of these three leaders added pressure to an already intense period with expansions in governmental regulations, the physical space of the hospital itself, and rapidly moving changes in medical practice. A misstep by the organization would have a larger negative impact than in normal times.

What was worse, at such a moment when leadership was so vital for a steady navigation of choppy waters, Community Hospital had no succession plan for its formal leadership position. The organization had not laid out the pathway from a current executive administrator to a carefully chosen replacement. The absence of a succession plan deepened the shock of McLin's death, with only uncertainty and confusion—to say nothing of rumors—to fill the gap.

The moment had all the makings of organizational drift.

One fact proved of incalculable worth as the challenge of the three deaths unfolded: Community Hospital's culture, the ways in which the doctors, staff, and volunteers collectively worked, served, and interacted together. Though the publicity of McLin's death might have suggested that he had dominated the organization, the hospital's fundamental strength was its medical personnel, the doctors, nurses, and technicians. Doctors held a large number of seats of the board of directors, for example, nurses had widespread influence on every floor and in every department, and staff and technicians held a strong attachment to the nature of their work.

This culture kept the hospital's focus where its people believed it had always been—on the residents and families of surrounding neighborhoods, on the patients and their families who entered the doors off Ritter Avenue and Sixteenth Street to receive some of the best medical care available in the Midwest. Together with the efforts of hundreds of volunteers of the Women's Auxiliary and key support staff, the daily work of Community Hospital continued unabated.

So strong was the culture that Community Hospital's board of directors made an extraordinary decision in light of McLin's death. For the past three years McLin and the board had worked on another major building expansion. The plan was to add more than 300,000 square feet to the hospital. It would be an enormous undertaking. The demise of McLin was both a bad omen for starting such a large project and, in the face of the breach, a potential source of disagreement and misunderstanding for its implementation.

That's not how the board of directors saw things. With the hospital's doctors, nurses, staff, and volunteers staying resilient in the aftermath of McLin's passing, Walter Pagenkopf and the rest of the board voted to forge ahead with the building plan. Pagenkopt announced the $10 million project in August 1971 with a three-year timeline of completion. The board's action testified to boldness and determination as organizational values.

The announcement was a stunning move. Community Hospital's building plans blazed across newspaper headlines throughout Indianapolis. Articles highlighted the proportional increase in space, with 261 beds "that almost will double the size of the hospital." Lewis & Shimer Architects designed the new building to have "a square one-story base topped by a four-story cross-shaped structure." The building would cost $10 million and paid through a combination of federal funding, local bank loans, and commitment of hospital revenues.

The publicity of the new building in eastern Indianapolis and Marion County reflected a similar degree of excitement for what would happen in the structure. Scores of new beds would be available for children and adults needing mental health treatment, rehabilitation and orthopedic care, long-term care, and critical access care that included the city's first luxury private suite of rooms. Surgeries would receive a boost with new specially designed and arranged operating rooms, cystoscopic examination facilities, and space for teams of surgeon, nurses, and technical staff to consult and prepare for daily operations. New dining halls would be available, along with the finest offerings in menu selections. The project seemed more than space-doubled. It foretold of an even greater promise for an already revered pillar of Indianapolis.

The board pushed further ahead. Acting on the recommendation of assistant director Robert T. Clarke, the board authorized hiring the first social worker in the history of Community Hospital, Mrs. Russell Rifleman. Though many employees were already trying to help patients and their families in need, Rifleman's hiring showed that Community Hospital would develop professional procedures in providing counseling and other support.

As the work on the new building got underway, Federal Judge William Steckler, David Easlick, and the other twenty-three members of the board of directors had a second decision to make. Thomas Wilburn appeared a natural choice to move up from his vice presidential slot to the presidency, the next-in-line behind McLin. This was especially logical in the context of overseeing a vast new building project as well as the simplest solution for not having a succession plan. Amazingly, though, board members reached a consensus that the time had arrived for an even more intense pursuit of a new direction.

They wanted to hire an outsider, a formal leader with a fresh style and approach to the organization, perhaps an embodiment of the new phase in Community Hospital's history as symbolized in the building project. Wilburn acknowledged the turn in the board's thinking and left to become chief operating officer at Bethesda North in Cincinnati where he subsequently launched a new hospital and became a prominent health care leader. Community Hospital's board thanked Wilburn for his service and charged the senior executive team to take over interim presidential duties. From there, the board formed a sub-group to look more broadly for McLin's replacement. The search narrowed to a young man in Chicago.

He was Allen Hicks, 41 years old and, like McLin, an Iowa native. The similarities ended there. Hicks was McLin's opposite in many ways. He was gregarious, outgoing, ready to break out in smile or laughter at a second's notice, and possessed with boundless social energy. He relished people and his relationships with them. Hicks's first instinct upon entering a room was not to sit and think but rather to move and meet.

In addition to his amiability, Hicks was already a proven healthcare leader in Chicago. He was chief administrator at the Illinois Masonic Hospital and Medical Center in Chicago and the president of the Chicago Hospital Council, no small achievement in the nation's second largest metropolis. Active in the city's civic life, Hicks had recently won an award for community service and was a board member or president of such organizations as the United Fund, the Council on Extended Care, and the community relations committee of the American Hospital Association.

Hicks's background was varied. He had served in the US Navy during World War II and the Korean War. He had chosen to enter hospital management after giving serious consideration to careers in hotel management and city management. His hospital career in Illinois included the hosting of a six-day per week radio show broadcasted from his office. Hicks's hospital leadership in Chicago had included a working relationship with Democratic Mayor Richard Daley, one of the most hard-nosed urban politicians in the US.

In fall 1971, Community Hospital board chairman Walter Pagenkopf telephoned Hicks in Chicago and offered him the position as Community Hospital president. Hicks shocked Pagenkopf by declining the offer. Hicks liked his current job and loved Chicago, especially its professional football team, the Chicago Bears, where he had once been the team's medical coordinator. The city suited him well.

Disappointed but undaunted, Pagenkopf changed tactics. He posed a question to Hicks. He asked Hicks not to reject the offer definitively. He invited him to visit Indianapolis and spend time with Community Hospital's board of directors before making a final decision. Hicks agreed. Without stating it directly, Pagenkopf was gambling on the powerful appeal of both Community and the city of Indianapolis.

Over the next week Hicks traveled to Indianapolis and stayed near Community Hospital. Pagenkopf and the rest of the board members convened a special meeting to talk with Hicks. Also, smaller sub-groups of board members and separate individuals met with Hicks for private talks and tours of the hospital. Hicks had several long meetings with doctors on the board. Doctors constituted one-quarter of the board's membership, a point that left a visible impression on Hicks.

In these meetings Hicks heard the same things over and over: Community Hospital had a powerful sense of commitment from board members; Community Hospital was unique in the close-knit feeling shared by doctors, nurses, staff, and patients; and Community Hospital had done the unimaginable in the early 1950s by opening with grassroots and neighborhood-level fundraising and impressive growth since.

The result of this intensive exposure to Community Hospital, particularly his insights into the organization gained from meeting board members, convinced Hicks of one thing—his first decision was the wrong decision. After four days, Hicks met with Pagenkopf and told him he had changed his mind. He would accept the presidency of Community Hospital after all. The news delighted Pagenkopf and the board. Chicago's loss, Indianapolis's gain.

And on January 10, 1972, Allen Hicks walked into the president's office at Community Hospital for his first day on the job. There was a new chair behind the desk, courtesy of Pagenkopf and the hospital board. Pagenkopf and the board stated clearly their expectations of Hicks. Later, Hicks remembered the words vividly: "Don't raise money," they said, "Tell us what you want and we will raise it for you."

The Hicks era had begun.

Among Hicks's first discoveries was the nature of greater Indianapolis and Community Hospital's fit into the fabric of the city. By the time of Hicks's arrival, Indianapolis encompassed nearly all of Marion County as a political entity. It had grown into a significant Midwestern city. Yet coming from Chicago, Hicks found a different revelation—in a metropolis like Chicago, a hospital sought to survive, while in a smaller and more intimate city such as Indianapolis, there was an opportunity to be a thriving, healthy, and secure community member with reduced fears of failure. He saw that the organization was more than a medical building. Community Hospital was part of the human landscape of both a section of the city and the larger city itself. Hicks quickly grew to embrace living in Indianapolis and that fact heightened his appreciation for Community Hospital, one of the city's precious resources.

As a newcomer, Hicks had to deepen his initial impressions of the organization. He described the hospital as "tip-top" and "in great shape." He judged that the strong connection between the board of directors and the hospital resulted in large part from the presence of so many doctors as board members. It was a very rare circumstance, Hicks concluded. The consistent involvement of doctors with patients, support staff, caregivers, and administrators produced a cohesion and unity across the hospital. It was a precious resource.

Besides the imprint from the doctors, Hicks learned that almost everyone in the hospital could tell a story from the fundraising effort in the early 1950s. By the time of his arrival, nearly twenty years after the founding, Hicks realized that the story echoed on every floor, in every unit. The story helped the people who worked at Community Hospital know who they were as a group. The story gave the organization a face, a body, an identity. The fundraising memory predated McLin, the hospital's first executive, and such was its strength that Hicks understood he had to form his own leadership around it. When anyone reflected on the history of Community, the word story was automatically embedded in it, and the story was always the same—the fundraising of the founding.

The power of the founding story posed a challenge to Hicks. Left alone, the memories—and myths—of the founding story could take on a life of their own and prevent change and improvement. The founding story gave the status quo a sanctity that might prove destructive in the long run. Hicks was grateful and respectful of the origins and past of Community Hospital, however, he also recognized the need for new approaches. He saw in front of him a tightrope—embracing the hospital's existing tradition while still striving to seek progress and new gains.

He would have to walk that tightrope.

The path Hicks chose was communication. He observed a gap of interaction between the executive level of the hospital and the wider set of Community Hospital employees. Both groups shared common ground in the hospital's founding and its past, but they didn't speak directly to each other as much as Hicks thought they should. Here, then, was the device to balance his precarious steps.

He began a new method of interaction at Community Hospital. He started a formal process of meeting with employees every six months, usually over coffee. It required two weeks of constant meetings to be able to sit down with almost every member of the staff. Since this was new, the first set of these six-month rounds emphasized the upcoming half-year. After that, Hicks's meetings looked both backward and forward; the employee would update him on what had happened in the previous half-year and then discuss what he or she hoped or expected to occur the following six months.

Hicks's approach to communication was so effective in the employee meetings that he decided to use it throughout the hospital. Building on a naturally engaging personality, Hicks likened himself to a church pastor—a sort of health care organizational evangelist—whose first duty was to listen to the congregation. He admitted freely that "I'm the outsider and the employees know a lot more things than I do." The style endeared him to employees throughout Community Hospital.

Hicks established for himself and his executive team a clear list of priorities. He stated that the keys to their success would be maintaining good relations with the medical staff, keeping in close touch with the surrounding community, seeking out the input of board members, and serving as trusted financial stewards of all types of resources. If the organization's leaders did these four things, Community Hospital would not only maintain its status within Indianapolis but would also expand its pre-eminence in central Indiana and beyond.

One of Hicks's early decisions was to promote Robert Clarke from a position as McLin's assistant to a formal vice presidency. Clarke excelled at interacting with staff, guiding key projects, and handling autonomy and initiative with a sense of duty. As time went on, Clarke rose to an executive vice presidency that included the supervision of relations with medical staff and oversight of operations. Clarke hired almost half of the twenty-six medical department directors. His record justified Hicks's instincts and his trust. Hicks and Clarke became a remarkable pair.

With Allen Hicks, the second formal leader at Community Hospital, now comfortably in place, the organization rounded the bend and headed into a new future.

CHAPTER 6
An Upward Feeling, 1972-1978

A feeling of freshness swirled around Community Hospital after the early 1970s. The arrival of Allen Hicks was part but not all of it. The freshness came too from the growing relationship between Hicks and the hospital's caregivers and volunteers, and from the board of trustees' launch of the building project. A new period of healthcare dawned for the people who worked and served and were cared for at the hospital along Ritter Avenue.

The reality of a fresh start was blurred during the spring of 1972. On Mother's Day, May 14, a tornado ripped through the eastern part of Marion County and nearby Hancock County. More than thirty people were injured in the powerful storm, ten of whom were treated at Community Hospital's emergency room. For Hicks, the jolting event illustrated the bond between the hospital and the surrounding neighborhoods, towns, and villages.

A different sort storm slowed progress on the new building. Arguments and disagreements between the carpenter's union and contractors boiled over into a strike. The labor walk-out delayed work on Community Hospital's unfinished facility. The executive team had to adjust plans for offering new services that were part of the expansion.

The sense of a second beginning, however, would not be denied. The board of Community Hospital named its first honorary director,

George A. Kuhn Sr. Kuhn had been on the original board and was one of the inspirational leaders of the hospital development commission when Community was founded. Kuhn's selection as the first honorary director signaled that any short-term turmoil over construction stood in the shadows of a long and rich organizational past.

Still looking ahead beyond temporary setbacks, Community nurses Rosemary Walter and Jane Bailey led the work of starting a new sub-department among the nurses, rehabilitative nursing. Walter and Bailey convinced Hicks and the executive team, who in turn convinced the board of trustees, that the new specialization among nurses would meet a critical need among residents of eastern Indianapolis and central Indiana. The program testified to the energy and commitment of Community's nurses.

The impressive record of Community nurses was a key reason behind the continued success of the partnership with Indiana Central College (University of Indianapolis). By early 1973, the student nursing program at the college had its highest graduating class ever, with a core element of their clinical education occurring at Community. The college chose Allen Hicks to be the featured speaker at the nurses' graduation ceremony. Hicks gave his speech to the nurses shortly before receiving another educational honor, this time having been named a faculty member to the School of Medicine at Indiana University-Purdue University Indianapolis.

The spirit of innovation began to accelerate throughout Community Hospital. Inspired by their success with the university nursing partnership, Community's nurses developed a statewide "refresher" program for nurses to become better versed in the latest medical research and techniques. Trained volunteers opened a "Senior Citizen Information Center" that advised elderly patients and residents on how to use assistance programs offered by community groups, churches as well as federal, state, and local governments. Even the hospital chaplain, William Hogsett, was swept up in the innovative spirit. Hogsett designed a free educational seminar based on the then-best selling psychology book on transcendental meditation, "I'm OK, You're OK", by Thomas Harris.

Community Hospital's immersion in change and new beginnings

extended into deeply controversial public issues. These issues pointed to the wider effects of government policy on the hospital. President Richard Nixon—the former Vice-President under Eisenhower and keynote speaker at the ground-breaking ceremony of the hospital back in 1954—had recently issued an executive order freezing all wages and prices for a 90-day period. Nixon as President was far more willing to involve the federal government in economic affairs than Nixon as Vice-President two decades before.

Nixon's order outraged many employees at Community Hospital. They made their anger known to Hicks during his regular rounds of communication with staff. True to form, Hicks responded—he directed his vice-president for finance to add a ten-percent bonus to the retirement accounts of each employee. The bonus circumvented Nixon's regulations. Personnel director William Curtis met with small groups of employees to explain the change.

Hicks, his executive team, and the Community Hospital board of trustees discussed the real possibility that Nixon's wage-cap decision had placed the hospital on the verge of a crisis. The rising chances of a severe upward spike in gasoline prices—nations in the Middle East had just formed an oil cartel to raise prices—left the board fearful that Nixon would embark on further centralized economic planning.

The furor tightened the relationship between Hicks and one of his crucial advisors, the hospital's legal counsel, Leonard Betley. Soft-spoken and modest, Betley belonged to the law firm of Ice Miller and provided legal guidance to Hicks and Community Hospital. Hicks huddled with regularly with Betley as the hospital traversed the thickets of federal government regulations and restrictions.

Hicks contacted his acquaintences in Washington DC to express his and the board's misgivings. Hicks had known Illinois Congressman Everitt Dirksen, former Speaker of the House of Representatives. Though Dirksen had died a few years earlier, Hicks had maintained relationships with several political figures in Congress. Using these back-channels of communication as well as month-to-month changes in Medicare and Medcaid policies, Hicks believed that the prospects for much greater involvement of the federal government in business and the economy was in the offing. He did not relish the possibility.

In addition, Community Hospital reacted to the new U.S. Supreme Court ruling, Roe v. Wade, that struck down all abortion laws across the nation. Dr. Robert Arnold was instrumental in establishing new procedures and processes for Community Hospital patients who wished to obtain an abortion. Arnold and other doctors were prepared to receive additional patients seeking abortions and wanted the hospital to have a studied, research-based approach to meet the rise in demand.

More innovation occurred in 1973. Community Hospital opened a mental health outpatient clinic along with two satellite facilities in nearby Hancock and Shelby Counties. Led by newly installed director Mike Peterson, the clinic's funding emerged from state taxes, patient fees, and community donations; President Richard Nixon had just eliminated federal money for mental health centers. The clinic invoked memories of the founding of Community Hospital with its independence from federal government funds. The new clinic was a footprint for a larger new mental health program the following year.

Honoring Edward Gallahue, the Gallahue Mental Health Clinic was the embodiment of Community Hospital's founding connection to the needs of local patients. Gallahue's mother had suffered from depression, and the new Clinic immediately became one of Indiana's stellar resources in the treatment of mental illness. Perhaps the most outstanding component of the Clinic was a path-breaking adolescent psychiatric unit. A dozen beds were in the unit, reserved for youth ages thirteen to seventeen who faced challenging mental illnesses. If necessary, they would be able to reside in the unit for up to eight weeks. The program, the only one of its kind within the 36-county region of central Indiana, was led by Dr. Robert Pearce.

Paired with the new mental health clinic was one of the biggest innovations in recent history at Community Hospital. The August J. Hook Rehabilitation Center, a 72-bed facility would open in 1974. The center, assistant director Donald Sibery said, "is an elaboration of what we already have." Sibery was referring to a fifteen-year record in rehabilitative care and the newly offered nursing specialization in rehabilitation.

Beyond the sheer size of the thing, the center's uniqueness rested on three features. First, the center would have a full-time medical director with an expertise in rehabilitative medicine, known as a physiatrist. Second, the beds used for patients were specifically designed for rehabilitative treatments. Third and perhaps most importantly, this would be the most broadly constructed rehabilitation program in Indiana. The program encompassed strong partnerships with existing agencies, including Goodwill, Crossroads, and the Indiana Rehabilitation Center. Sibery stated, "One of the key problems which we now hope to resolve through our new center is to provide patients with full access into a statewide system of comprehensive care." Before now, Indiana residents needed rehabilitative services had to travel to New York, Illinois, or Texas to access the few such offerings in the nation. Community's new program was a critical addition to this capacity.

The center also offered a unique approach to health and wellness. Pioneered by Community's Dr. Charles White and Dr. Karl Manders, the center concentrated on holistic medicine. The focal point of care was not just the patient but the entirety of the patient's condition and well-being. Stress, attitude, demeanor, and more, the holistic approach of White and Manders sought to reduce the dependency on both pharmaceutical treatments and narrowly specialized procedures. "The medical model," Manders stated, "has to change so that the delivery of healthcare is not so much to an organ as to the person." Dr. Jerry Wesch, Community Hospital's director of medical psychology, agreed, asserting that this and other new trends toward prevention and wellness stood to redefine the foundation of medicine.

Hicks saw the center as a fascinating probe into the future of medicine and healthcare. He supported the innovative techniques of White and Manders, while at the same time was cautious about expanding the scale to entire communities, states, and the nation itself. He was also unsure about the connection between outcomes and pricing, something that anticipated tensions that would boil over in health care forty years later.

Allen Hicks further viewed the rehabilitation center as an important collaboration between Community and one of the most visible Indiana-based companies at the time, Hook's Drug Store Inc. Hook's was known for its extensive involvement in projects in several central Indiana towns and neighborhoods. The rehabilitation center fit perfectly with Hicks's desire to tighten relationships between Community Hospital and influential Indiana-oriented businesses.

Also opening in 1974 was an expanded and revamped set of emergency rooms, another product of the new building. Where the old facility had dark tile and poor lighting, the new emergency rooms featured sparkling lights and shining white tiling. Where the old emergency facility had eight rooms, the new emergency rooms numbered fourteen. In addition to the fourteen-room space, the emergency department had still more rooms for additional procedures, including pre-operative care and preparation for patients needing immediate surgery. Community Hospital's new emergency department became an attraction for medical students and newly licenced doctors.

Community's expanded building spawned a new firm that grew into a nationally renowned healthcare engineering and architectural company. Thirty-four year-old Richard Sobieray was one of the designers of the expanded facility, part of Lewis & Shimer Architects. Sobieray's experience on the project convinced him to launch his own venture, partnering with Dwight Boyd. Allen Hicks admired Sobieray's work and his nature, and helped him gain confidence as a new business owner. The new firm, soon known as BSA Life Structures, would have key roles in healthcare building design throughout the United States.

For Community Hospital, the impressive facility of 1974 was a physical sign of new patterns in healthcare. The doctors and staff at Community Hospital were treating people through shorter stays and faster medical procedures, a response to pressure from insurance companies and federal and state government regulators alike. In just a five-year span in the 1970s, Community Hospital had slashed the time a heart attack patient occupied a patient room from fifteen days to nine days. Emergency rooms and outpatient treatment were emerging as key factors at Community Hospital.

These pressures had their costs, too. A group of anesthesiologists at Community Hospital were denied standard malpractice insurance in late 1974. The insurance company that normally—and uneventfully—supplied the coverage suddenly cut off the doctors's access to medical plans. The issue at hand was cost; the purchase price for malpractice insurance had risen in a single year from $100,000 to almost $1,000,000 for Community Hospital. Allen Hicks threatened to shut down the hospital's entire surgical program unless the company reinstated the doctors and scaled back rates to previous levels. The company refused. Furious over the decision, Hicks huddled with various state insurance regulators and legislators. Shortly before the end of year, Hicks announced that a second insurance company had agreed to provide one-year coverage to the anesthesiologists. The incident reflected the significant power of insurance companies in the changing day-to-day reality of healthcare for Community Hospital. It also foretold of potential ruptures to come.

These trends did not distract the people of Community Hospital from their fundamental purpose and culture. The Women's Auxiliary, presided over by Mrs. Arthur Ecklund, maintained their intense schedule of activities on the hospital's behalf. The red geranium sale in the spring, the boutique in the autumn, and dozens of other events raised significant resources for equipment, the health careers scholarship program, and the financial aid program for indigent patients. Volunteers racked up thousands of hours, with Irene Jeffries by herself accounting for more than 10,000 hours of service annually.

If anything, the changes and intensifying pressures in healthcare induced Community Hospital to rely even more on those values that had guided the organization for nearly a quarter-century. The Women's Auxiliary exemplified the trend. In addition to their traditional work, these dedicated volunteers organized a detailed cancer awareness workshop. The workshop included descriptions and guides to the latest findings in cancer research and tips on best-practices in diet and behavior. Like the Hook Rehabilitation Center, the Women's Auxiliary was attuned to innovations that were altering healthcare.

Moreover, in 1976, slightly over a year since the new building's completion, a committee within Community Hospital announced the creation of an entirely new medical education initiative, the Family Medicine Residency Program (FMRP). The FMRP grew organically out of the hospital's deep roots in family medical practices across the eastern half of Marion County. Allen Hicks viewed the program as a way to "train the medical staff in a way unique to our organization" and to bring cohesion to "the many family doctors who wanted to be independent and outside of centralized authority." Hicks asserted the program would help ensure that the primary medical education effort in Indiana—operated by the Indiana University School of Medicine—would only add to the medical culture of Community Hospital, not overrun it.

Dr. Robin Ledyard, a graduate of the FMRP, stated that the program enabled young doctors to "get to know each other and develop a collective identity... They developed a connection that made them want to stay at Community." As Hicks foresaw, Ledyard attested to the program's strong effect on "encouraging the attitude that we are living out our values and the value of relationships on a day-to-day basis." From its inception, more than half of medical students completing the FMRP ultimately decided to remain with Community Hospital. FMRP was a leadership garden for Community Hospital, eventually growing such organizational leaders as Dr. Paul Wilson, Dr. Cliff Knight, and countless others.

The FMRP epitomized the broader medical education at Community. Whether as interns, externs, or formal participants in the FMRP, Community's doctors went out of their way to involve medical students in meaningful medical learning. David Kiley recalled the learning experience at Community as uniquely intense, a blend of practical decision-making, clinical analysis, and delegated responsibility. Don Ziperman praised the mission-like zeal of doctors and nurses alike who nurtured the emerging independence of scores of aspiring physicians. Rod Corson compared the learning culture at the hospital to a life-molding experience, an exposure to doctor-teachers who were "like heroes to me."

The cluster of innovation and change within Community Hospital generated a magnetic effect within the surrounding region. Building on a nine-point plan developed by Indianapolis Mayor Richard Lugar, Indiana's legislature enacted a law to organize a 30-county planning region for health services in 1975. The plan and the law sought to improve the efficiency of using resources at Community Hospital and other medical facilities in central Indiana. The belief was that greater efficiency would assist Community Hospital and other organizations as they struggled to adapt to the bewildering blend of more demand for quality service, tightening budgets, increased regulation, and funamental changes in population and the economy.

An interesting choice was made for how to proceed to staff the 30-county planning organization. Indiana lawmakers determined that Allen Hicks should be the point of coordination for identifying the best person to oversee the initiative. The choice of Hicks illustrated the widely held view that Community Hospital was a healthcare cornerstone for eastern Marion County and surrounding towns and villages. It further emphasized the confidence that many political and civic leaders had in Allen Hicks as a man committed to the public good and to a broad vision of organizational collaboration.

Strikingly, a second endorsement of a similar nature occurred soon thereafter. In another endeavor to harness resources across organizational lines, Indianapolis leaders in government, business, and community services launched the nation's first regional advisory board for placing physically disabled people in workplaces. Once again, Community Hospital was the first call made by the program's advocates—a regional affiliate of a national organization known as Mainstream. Mainstream's local representatives needed a clear idea as to how best to proceed with finding employment opportunities for disabled residents.

There was a lot at stake in this instance. Mainstream's spokespersons hinted that if enough jobs weren't found, a high-profile protest would be held to publicize any resistance the disabled might have encountered in Indianapolis, complete with wheel-chair protestors attempting to enter targeted buildings. Such a warning wasn't idle—public protests against the Vietnam War, on behalf of civil rights, and in favor of various social causes were the norm for American communities by the mid-1970s. Fortunately for the city, Allen Hicks and the staff at Community Hospital were eager to help advise on the best possibilities for jobs and works. Hicks met with Mainstream officials and assured them of his and Community Hospital's genuine support for the effort. A forward-thinking reputation was firmly in place at Community Hospital.

By 1976, Community Hospital's visibility across greater

Indianapolis was growing at a rapid rate. A sense of momentum existed. A feeling of excitement and enthusiasm swirled around the organization. A member of Hicks's executive team, Robert Shaw, compared the organizational climate to the "Camelot" feeling of the John Kennedy presidency; Camelot was a fictitious tale from medieval England where nobility, progress, and optimism were common qualities. The upbeat at Community Hospital laid down a choice in front of Allen Hicks and other hospital leaders on Ritter Avenue. What to do with the momentum?

Here was an intriguing question. A reasonable answer was to do nothing unusual. Community Hospital could enjoy the momentum, its doctors, nurses, and staff continuing to care for patients, working hard in a volatile healthcare environment. The present state of affairs argued that the best strategy was to keep doing what was already succeeding.

But that wasn't Community Hospital's way and that wasn't Allen Hicks's way. Hicks's idea was to use the momentum as a planting ground for the hospital's fundraising. He wanted to expand the foundation—which had begun operating in 1961 as an internal holding capacity for modest donations—and transform it into a fuller, stronger, and better equipped fundraising arm of the hospital. This new version of the foundation would be more visible across Marion County and the rest of central Indiana. Here was yet another reason why one observer called Hicks "the engine that stoked up the hospital."

On May 17, 1976, Hicks announced the formation of the Community Hospital Foundation (CHF). William Dyer, president of Indianapolis Newspapers Inc, stepped forward as the first chairperson of the newly revamped CHF. August Hook of Hooks Drug Stores and Harry Ice of Ice, Miller, Donadio, and Ryan law firm rounded out the members of CHF's executive committee. Additional CHF board members included Eugene Hibbs, Frank Hoke, Dr. Raymond Rice, William Spurlock, Mrs. Harvey Bradley, Richard De Mars, Dr. James Denney, Otto Frenzel Sr, Mrs. Clarence Hamilton, Dr. Roy Geider, James Gloin, George Varnes, and Dr. Malcolm Wrege. Like the hospital's board of directors, this group mixed influential business people with doctors and medical staff of high standing.

Community Hospital Chaplain William Hogsett took over duties of running CHF. Under Hogsett's leadership, CHF's purpose was "to raise funds for new equipment, education programs and new services at Community Hospital." The prestigious roster of board members combined with the new expectation of public visibility to make CHF as significant new entity at Community Hospital.

The reputation of Community Hospital for seeking innovation and change and accepting the risk that comes with both reached a new level by 1976. The clash with the insurance company over malpractice costs, combined with the stronger directives from government regulators, convinced Hicks and much of the hospital's leadership that bold steps needed to be taken.

From his office on Ritter Avenue, Hicks looked southward for an astonishly creative solution to the insurance problem. Hicks obtained approval from the board of trustees to establish, in sunny Bermuda, the Multihospital Mutual Insurance Company (MMI) in 1976. MMI was Hicks's attempt to avoid the tight control that insurance companies had on Community Hospital and other healthcare organizations. The board agreed that Hicks would serve as MMI's executive officer, offering affordable malpractice insurance to Community Hospital's doctors and also to medical staff at participating hospitals. The location in Bermuda was a way of attracting doctors and adapting to different organizational requirements on the off-shore island.

Hicks and Community Hospital adopted the two-part formula again a year later. Using the experience with off-shore organizational practices and a collaborative structure, Hicks began discussions with colleagues from other hospitals on founding a group-purchase entity that could help member-hospitals cut their shared costs. Hicks crafted the concept with three hospital-executive colleagues, Pat Groner and M.T. Mustian from Florida and Duncan Moore from Iowa. "They were high-octane, enthusiastic people who were not afraid to step out and make a decision," Hicks said, "and they had the enthusiasm that goes with leaders who make things happen." From these talks came a plan of action for a new external enterprise, the second in as many years for Community Hospital.

Characteristically, Hicks volunteered to seek out additional partners to join the core of this new venture. He met with Stanley Nelson from Michigan and Wade Mountz from Kentucky. Hicks persuaded them to participate. By 1977, an initial collaboration of thirty hospitals had been developed, known as Voluntary Hospitals of America (VHA).

Hicks was careful to explain to Community Hospital staff and to the Women's Auxiliary about the new entity. Without a precise understanding of VHA's aims, a risk existed that rumors would spread about Community Hospital losing its identity and unique sense of purpose. Hicks's remarks to these audiences laid out the case for stabilizing the finances of Community Hospital. He spoke about navigating the stormy environment of insurance companies, federal government regulators, and other powerful stakeholders. The hospital balanced a mix of revenue sources that included 33% from government, 25% from public insurers, 25% from private insurers, and only 17% from private payers (the most among Indianapolis hospitals).

VHA registered as a corporation in Delaware in 1977 but operated in the Grand Cayman Islands before relocating to Dallas, Texas. It quickly became a nationally known entity for its ability to enable member-hospitals to cut costs and conduct group purchasing in the non-clinical aspects of operating a hospital. By Hicks's own estimate, most hospitals devoted seventy-five percent of their budgets to labor costs; the primary savings had to come from non-labor items that VHA helped provide on a shared basis. Within a short time, Hicks also served as president of VHA and oversaw the segmentation of the enterprise into distinctive lines of activity, such as VHA Enterprises, VHA Supply, and VHA Physician Services.

Because of Hicks's position within VHA, Community Hospital used its affiliation to the enterprise for maximum benefit. VHA provided shared research and managerial services to Community Hospital, along with computer technology and other equipment. Hicks saw to it that Community Hospital retained complete autonomy, independence, and identity within the national organization.

While Hicks agreed to serve as treasurer for VHA, several of Community Hospital's doctors worked on selected assignments for the organization. They provided assessment and evaluation services, enabled the staffs of member-hospitals to share best practices in numerous aspects of healthcare, and maintained a robust flow of information in medical specializations scattered across different hospitals in the US. One of the participating doctors from Community Hospital, Dr. Rod Corson, stated that the activity also continued to strengthen the bonds that the doctors had with each other and with all of Community Hospital. VHA was, Corson said, "one of the many reasons it was exciting to be part of all that was going on at Community Hospital. You knew that you were part of something that drew a lot of awareness from throughout the US. You knew it was special."

This sense of being at a "special" place and doing "special" work for patients healthcare enabled Community Hospital to push ahead despite the tensions in healthcare. It was this sense that continued to attract people of the highest caliber to Community Hospital's workforce by the end of 1977. Allen Hicks depended on this sense to help convince such emerging healthcare leaders as Dr. Glenn Bingle to leave his position at Henry Ford Hospital in Detroit and become the director of medical education. In the future, Dr. Bingle would earn a reputation as one of the hospital's most committed leaders.

But before that would happen, the new year of 1978 would dawn, and before the first month of that year was over, on January 24, the temperature had dropped below freezing. What was rain a day earlier was now turning to snow. The next few days would be etched in the memories of the people at Community Hospital.

CHAPTER 7
Standing Strong, 1978-1981

No one at Community Hospital, no one in Indianapolis, and no one in central Indiana had ever seen anything like it.

In the final week of January 1978 a winter storm gathered power in southern Canada and over the Great Lakes and roared into Indiana and greater Indianapolis. With blinding snow and relentless winds, the Great Blizzard of 1978, as it was soon called, came to be one of the most important collective experiences in the history of Community Hospital. Over a 96-hour period, the modern life known to every doctor, nurse, staff member, and patient at Community Hospital ground to a halt. Nature's fury blasted a hole in daily life.

A rain that had pelted Indianapolis during Wednesday, January 25, suddenly turned to snow as the following day unfolded. Temperatures plunged to 0 degrees Fahrenheit. Winds howled at speeds of more than fifty miles per hour. In Indianapolis that day, the storm created conditions where people could see no further than the end of their hand; the Indianapolis airport closed immediately as winds lashed across the landscape and enormous snow drifts began to rise. The blizzard stretched over the entire Great Lakes and Upper Midwest. It was, an observer noted, a hurricane in winter.

The mayor of Indianapolis, William Hudnut, announced a state of emergency for both the city and Marion County. City streets were deserted. Newspapers and trash blew in the high winds. Street signs shook, lashed with ice and snow. Thick coats of ice formed on windows and street lights, power lines sagged and swayed under the weight. Interstate highways, including I-465 that encircled Indianapolis, were clogged with hundreds of cars and trucks stuck in snowdrifts. Abandoned vehicles littered the streets and avenues near Community Hospital. Those who remained with their car or truck were at risk of frostbite and worse. With winds blasting at nearly speeds of seventy-five miles per hour, to be outside of a heated and secured structure was to be in dire physical danger.

For hours at a time, a constant roaring sound filled the air and white waves of snow ripped horizontally across the sky. It was a storm of unrivaled force—whether before or since—that drove people to seek safety inside their homes, places of work, or emergency shelters. It was a wintry version of the Dust Bowl from the Great Depression.

It was as if winter was at war with Hoosiers. Indiana Governor Otis Bowen responded with a declaration that all of Indiana was under a state of emergency. Bowen wanted to view conditions across the state but had to wait for the fierce winds to recede before he could safely board a helicopter. Hudnut's only form of travel was on a snow plow. Other political leaders compared the effect on transportation to the fallout of a nuclear explosion.

Members of the Indiana National Guard raced into action to rescue the people isolated along I-465 in Marion County. Armored personnel carriers normally deployed in wartime settings were used to rescue those stranded people. Other roads were shut down which hadn't been closed since they were created; some colleges and universities canceled entire days of classes for their first time in their history, while K-12 schools commenced a stretch of closures that lasted for days.

The rate of physical harm mounted. With wind-chill temperatures sinking to fifty degrees below zero Fahrenheit, severe frostbite and exposure were among the first signs of injury. Heart attacks began to multiply as people struggled to open driveways and pathways that the blizzard covered over again in a matter of minutes. Snowdrifts piled up ten feet high. Broken or twisted ankles and legs resulted from people who couldn't see through the blizzard stumbling into potholes of ice inside the twenty inches of snow on the ground.

Community Hospital, like other hospitals in the region, became a sort of fortress in the three-day siege. Doctors, nurses, and staff were unable to travel along streets and roads closed by the snow and by the public emergency orders. Along with the patients, they had to hole up in the hospital to ride out the storm.

Not everybody who was needed was there. Some patients depended on particular doctors and specialists for their care. "It's an all-round emergency," a Community Hospital employee said, "We're using a lot of volunteers and police to get doctors and key employees in." Out they went into the neighborhoods of eastern Indianapolis and Marion County to retrieve the practicioners who were vital to critically ill patients in the hospital. Once at the homes of these Community Hospital caregivers, they found professionals dressed and ready to go for the dangerous trip back to the hospital.

At Community Hospital itself, as in any siege, supplies began to run low. Food, medicines, and other items were stretched thin. Sleep and rest were in equally short supply. People who worked at Community Hospital had to join together into informal teams to do tasks that weren't part of their normal jobs: laundry had to be gathered and washed; beds had to be stripped and re-made; patient gowns and nurse uniforms had to be cleaned; dishes, cups, and pans required scouring. The tasks of work piled up, respecting no one's job description. Everyone pitched in.

Among the tasks were surgical operations. The external presence of the blizzard didn't affect the schedule of surgeries. If patients needed surgery, they got it regardless of the shortage of supplies. Again in ways that resembled a war-zone, the cases with the most critical needs received top priority in logistical and material support. If surgeons and surgical nurses were tired, too bad—the operations had to be performed despite the blizzard pounding on the windows of the Twin Towers.

These stalwart Community Hospital employees had still more than daily tasks and surgeries on their hands. Patients could sense the scale of the storm, especially the elderly, who might often harken back to their youth in the 1930s and 1940s and times of struggle and deprivation. They were increasingly anxious about their families back home or, worse yet, perhaps left stranded in the brutal conditions trying to visit the hospital. The band of employees had to calm the patients, updating them on efforts by city, county, and state officials to open the roadways and help those in need.

A striking effect took hold. With Community's buildings surrounded by the fierce winter storm and supplies dwindling within, caregivers feared a gap could arise, a gap between the needs of people inside the hospital and the medical material available to assist them. In some moments, such a gap might produce panic or despair. In this moment, however, Community Hospital's caregivers and staff responded with extra compassion, concern, and kindness. Patients reacted to them with their own warmth and affection. The bond between people inside the hospital, which was always strong, somehow became even stronger. Rather than seeing the worse, the reality of the challenge enabled people to see the best of themselves.

Employees who lived in surrounding neighborhoods could envision the conditions at besieged Community Hospital. Summoned by their work ethic and commitment to the shared experience of the hospital, several employees climbed aboard snow plows operated by street crews and rode to the hospital. Another employee owned a snowmobile; a set of fellow employees perched on the back of the machine and together they skidded along the ice-covered pavement to 16th Street and Ritter Avenue. Still others loaded into four-wheel drive trucks, their rugged tires tearing through the deep snow.

Some Community employees ventured the other way. They knew of local people who lived in poverty near the hospital and worried for their safety. These nearby residents, often elderly and of modest means, risked serious harm inside their houses if water pipes froze or heating units failed. Leaving Community Hospital but keeping in close contact with those still in the building, a group of Community Hospital employees braved the blizzard to carry food, knock on doors, and check on residents who might otherwise have gone without care or nourishment.

Those employees did bring some of the residents back with them to Community Hospital. They did so in order to ensure that the residents had food, water, and heat and, if needed, could receive a medical examination for a condition caused by the storm. These were informal emergency-medicine runs that helped prevent further health problems in the neighborhoods around 16th Street and Ritter Avenue.

The good deeds produced an unforeseen problem. People rescued by the employees' informal emergency-medicine runs had no way to return home. The difficulty in travel and the shortage in personnel made it impossible to organize a system to get them back to their houses and apartments.

The handful of staff trying to keep Community Hospital going didn't have the time, energy, or resources to resolve the issue. Their answer was to endure; their solution was to keep the retrieved residents at Community Hospital until the blizzard stopped. That meant Community's lobby and waiting rooms were overflowing with caregivers and local residents alike sleeping on sofas, chairs, and makeshift cots. They often ate or showered in shifts. Some of these folks smoked—cigarettes quickly disappeared and couldn't be restocked. This amounted to an improvised smoking ban. For some, it was one of the longest periods without a cigarette in their adult lives.

Allen Hicks saw the lobby and waiting rooms as examples of bigger problems. He was concerned that if the blizzard continued into a fifth or sixth day, a potential food shortage could slide into an actual lack of food.

Hicks's concern reflected an additional point about the storm. The situation had two components—one was the storm as it existed, the other was the aftermath of the storm, when it no longer existed but such effects as clogged streets and inoperable vehicles remained in place.

The first component was addressed when the storm dissipated by Monday, January 30. The second component, however, was only just beginning. There were roads to be dug out, stranded vehicles to be towed, homes to be opened up, and when the thaw commenced, flooding to be sand-bagged and cleaned up.

The beginning of February was the beginning of life returning to normal at Community Hospital. While eleven people died across Indiana, no lives had been lost at or around Community Hospital, and no serious injuries suffered. The improvisation, the sacrifice, the volunteerism, the just-pitch-in-and-do-it spirit that had permeated the entire hospital, all of it marked the four-day ordeal of Community Hospital during the worst winter storm in Indiana's recorded history. The siege was lifted. The siege was won.

Allen Hicks had both the self-awareness and group-awareness to know that a major event had just engulfed the people at 16th Street and Ritter Avenue. He wanted to express to the community of Indianapolis his pride in the people of Community Hospital. He also wanted to help the same tight-knit community of doctors, nurses, staff, patients, and of equal importance, the residents around them, to begin to have a clearer understanding of what had just happened. They had not only lived through something together, they had lived out something together, something with a larger meaning that Hicks believed should be better known.

Other healthcare leaders in Indianapolis had a similar idea. On February 7 Indiana University Hospital director Roger Hunt published a letter in the Indianapolis Star. A few days later, after organizing his thoughts, Hicks did the same. The two healthcare leaders shared the belief that the people of Indianapolis had done stellar work in assisting the hospitals; Hicks and Hunt expressed their gratitude. Beyond that, though, their letters diverged, yielding an interesting insight into the uniqueness of Community Hospital as an organization.

Hunt's letter was longer, and included details about specific efforts by street workers, public safety officers, and others. Hunt was dramatic, stating that his hospital had barely "survived" the storm's assault. He concluded in a flourish, confessing that he and his employees had had their confidence renewed in the people of Indianapolis. The inference was that such confidence might have been waning, might have been less evident, prior to the storm.

Hicks took a very different approach in his letter. His writing was spare and compact. He came straight to the point. "I would like to take this opportunity," he began, "to say thank you to all persons who assisted us at Community Hospital during the recent blizzard." Hicks sought to inform and remind everyone of the high stakes involved in the storm: "The responsibility for caring for 800 patients, many of whom are critically ill, is a great one and requires many hands," he explained. No happy outcome was guaranteed; many people were at risk. The blizzard was an extreme display of the kind of hazards that faced Community Hospital every day.

Hicks then turned to outlining the circles of support. He described the numerous sources of success achieved at the end of the day. He stated, "Because of the extra effort of our dedicated employees and doctors, the generosity of a great many volunteers, and the understanding and assistance of our patients and their families, we were able to provide continuous care." The powerful note that Hicks struck here was in listing people involved in producing the single, vital outcome of "care." Each member of the family of Community Hospital had played critical roles in the victory.

Hicks concluded with a telling assertion. "It was truly," he intoned, "a heroic effort by a great many people, and we are deeply grateful for everyone who assisted in keeping us going." For Hicks it was more about the straight-forward notion of "keeping us going" instead of the "survival" seen at another hospital. More importantly, Hicks bestowed a powerful award to the people around him—it was "heroism", a strong term, that—and the work and deeds of numerous folks who had earned the designation. Offered by Hicks in the sixth year of his tenure, this ending statement that linked "everyone" to "us" showed that he had fully absorbed the purpose of the organization. He didn't need his confidence in Indianapolis to be revived by the storm. Rather, the city and its people had given rise to Community Hospital more than twenty years ago. The blizzard of 1978 had simply reconfirmed what was already known at 16th Street and Ritter Avenue—Community Hospital was everyone, and everyone was Community Hospital. Community Hospital had emerged from the people and the city. The blizzard was just the latest and most dramatic display of bonds between the hospital and the place.

In the days and weeks that followed, the people of Community Hospital started the quiet process of not only returning to their work but also processing the Great Blizzard of 1978 into a shared memory. A bond was formed that would endure for decades to come. So strong was the bond that Anita Harden, one of Community Hospital's future leaders, having witnessed the impressive events at Community Hospital, decided to conduct formal research into the blizzard's effect on local healthcare. And forty years after the unprecedented winter storm, employees who had been at Community Hospital at the time recalled vividly their personal stories from that long-ago moment. They talked wistfully of the entire organization "coming together" and "just doing what needed to be done without complaint or agenda." For them the moment was magical, a fleeting state of best, a brief grasp of the ideal. They would always wish for the feelings of the Great Blizzard to swirl around their beloved Community Hospital.

In the two years that followed the Great Blizzard, Community Hospital provided major new services to its devoted patients, families, and partners. The Women's Auxiliary established a "Personal Alert Line" for elderly residents. Paying $8 a month, older citizens accessed a telephone line linked to Community Hospital volunteers and trained personnel for assistance in a personal health emergency. The hospital purchased a hyperbolic chamber to treat people with carbon monoxide poisoning, often a condition in homes where residents could not afford effective heating units. Also, Community replicated a program developed in Minnesota for educating cancer patients and their families on treatments; "I Can Cope" was the first such offering in Indiana. The Gallahue Mental Health Center at Community began a "Hug Station" where patients could request and receive a warm, personal hug from a volunteer or staff member. The Hug Station proved so popular that department directors across the hospital visited the Gallahue Center to see the program in action, taking turns in getting hugs.

Such programs, though small in scale, were part of Community's caring touch across greater Indianapolis. A hug in the hallway, a call at home, a suggestion on coping with severe illness, touches like these and a hundred others bonded families to Community over the years and miles of their lives. In September 1978, 28-year old Greg Ballard visited his father at Community Hospital on the day before young Ballard headed off to Officers Candidate School in the US Marine Corps. The elder Ballard had been a frequent patient at Community, battling severe arthritis much of his life. Father and son shared tender words in a room at Community on that late summer day, the elder Ballard choking back tears at saying goodbye to his youngest son. Years later, Greg Ballard, the retired Marine officer with a wife and children of his own would travel miles out of his way to receive care at Community during his term as Mayor of Indianapolis. Over two decades later, tears appeared again, this time in the son's memory of the moment spent with his father at Community.

Tears were shed in another Community room almost a year after the moment between the Ballards. On August 29, 1979, Kelly Ilene Guffen was born at Community Hospital. She was Ballard's opposite—weighing thirty ounces, the smallest baby ever born at Community down to that time. But like Ballard and so many thousands of other people, tiny Guffen found that Community Hospital was a part of her life, and her life was a part of Community Hospital. The trail of the burly Marine and the tiny infant ran through the hospital on 16th and Ritter.

If goodwill was money, Community Hospital was America's richest organization by the late 1970s. Community's service in the Great Blizzard and its responsive programs in the neighborhoods, the hospital was as vitally connected to the people around it as any time in its history. But larger strategic issues pressed hard on Community, demanding more than ever more from the organization. The costs of change were rising beyond anyone's control.

The local, state, and national economy of the late 1970s was sinking and showed no signs of relenting. High inflation added to high unemployment produced a new economic measurement: the misery index. In Indianapolis—especially eastern Indianapolis and eastern Marion County—the misery was indeed measurable. Businesses that had once been economic engines for well-paying manufacturing jobs had started to decline. Chrysler, Western Electric, Navistar, and others began to lose profitability, reduce their workforces, and perhaps worst of all, surrender confidence. Beneath the community of Community, the economic ground was quivering.

Prices for nearly everything at Community were going up; an increase in the value of silver led to large jumps in the cost of x-rays. Vice President of Finance Rex Smith asserted in late 1979 that Medicare's dominance of healthcare would expand to astonishing levels. Smith worried that patients and their families would be shocked when or if Community caregivers explained the unfolding reality of patient care. Officials from US President Jimmy Carter's administration told hospitals at a national healthcare conference that they would either have to cut costs drastically or face a rise in mandatory controls. The announcement was greeted by booing, jeering, and hissing from the crowd of hospital executives. Carter himself had gone on television to tell all Americans to turn down their thermostats and start wearing sweaters to keep warm.

Top leaders at Community Hospital responded to the widening economic crisis. Representatives from Community Hospital and Midtown Mental Health Center met with the City County Council to seek $500,000 in payments wrongfully made to another organization. Chief Financial Officer Rex Smith was especially adept at stabilizing payments from Medicare and Medicade, the two major funding sources from the federal government. Through Smith's skill, the hospital's pension plan stayed in good financial shape. And in an action that stirred media interest across Indiana, Don Vandergrift, Community's vice president for human resources, announced the decision to shift employees from Social Security to a company-administered retirement program.

Vandergrift's announcement reflected a decision by Allen Hicks and the board in late 1980 to participate in a nationally shared program for 400,000 non-profit employees. The shared retirement model offered Community a way to save money and give employees more discretion in personal finance. The departure from Social Security was a bold example of Community Hospital's willingness to take risks and innovate in response to major external demands.

Hard times didn't stop the people of Community Hospital from doing what they had done since founding. In 1980, one of Community's physicians, Dr. Patricia Keener, pregnant with her third child, determined that local mothers and baby-sitters didn't know how to save the lives of babies in such emergencies as choking. She had seen evidence of it in the hospital's emergency room. On her own, Keener designed a class to teach children and young parents how to save a choking baby. Within a few years, the program Keener started at Community had expanded onto a national platform. Almost two hundred lives were credited with being saved by her curriculum. Keener wrote dozens of protocols for Community, the hospital "she loved," according to a colleague.

1980 was the same year Carol Frantz hired on as a nurse at CHE. She quickly saw the inner workings of the hospital and was impressed. "Stream-lined, highly professional, and clearly focused the greatest effectiveness in caring for patients" was how she described CHE. The expectation was that clinical staff like Frantz needed to live no more than a half-hour from the hospital in order to respond to emergencies. They performed hard, physical work in lifting equipment and patients alike as well as hauling trash from patient rooms. Surgeries involved hand-worked drills, while fingers on pulses and stethascopes on chests were standard monitoring techniques. Older nurses told her they were working with patients in much the same way they had twenty years ago—making their own saline, using their own needle boxes for sutering with re-usable needles, working in the operating rooms in the morning and restocking items and preparing their needle bags later on for the next day's use.

These routines concealed a raw truth by early 1981. The scale of unknowns in health care had reached a crisis point for Community. Hicks and the board talked about the best strategy for the near-term future. The only thing anyone knew for certain was that uncertainty loomed ahead.

Side-by-side with intense economic pressures were ongoing needs for physical expansion and upgrades. Hicks and the boards of both the hospital and the hospital's foundation agreed on the importance of new laboratory and medical office space and targeted improvements of existing facilities. They decided to move forward. In so doing, they were diligent in seeking approval from people and groups who might have looked negatively on the project in such rough economic times. Community's leaders paid strict attention to gaining consensus first among surrounding neighborhoods (October 1979); then with local governmental agencies (January 1980); and finally with bond markets for the financing (February 1980). The result was the opening a year later in 1981 of a new professional medical building, a newly modernized lab, and other improvements. Despite economic strife, in a blend of insight, decisiveness, risk-taking, and action, Community Hospital expanded.

In early 1981 the newly elected President of the United States, Ronald Reagan, gave a stirring speech at his inauguration. In a ceremony that faced west from the US Capitol for the first time, Reagan admitted frankly that the sagging economy "threatens to shatter the lives of millions of our people." He called upon Americans to "act worthy of ourselves" and to "renew ourselves in our own land."

Within a time of despair, Community Hospital took up Reagan's challenge and charged ahead.

CHAPTER 8
A New World, 1981-1983

1981 was a year of celebration at Community Hospital. Staff and employees planned for an event to honor the hospital's 25th year in existence. Scheduled for later in the year, planners expected to invite the first baby born at the hospital—the public relations team would track down 25-year old Bryan and Bruce Grey—and also clear the hospital's main parking lot for a carnival, dunk tanks, and games. To commemorate the first quarter-century of service would be an excellent way to anticipate the next quarter-century stretching beyond the year 2000.

The rumblings of a bigger event, however, were just beginning. In spring 1981, Community Hospital confronted its biggest change since the first shovel dug into the dirt at 16th Street and Ritter Avenue. On the surface, the change didn't seem all that startling—it was about new buildings, new spaces, new square footage. These were familiar appearances of change that the doctors, nurses, staff, and stakeholders of Community had grappled with before.

No, the change about to occur struck more at the root of things, to the core question of: are we changing who we are?

The driver of this change was one of the most remarkable people in the history of the hospital, John W. Heiney. Known as "Jack" to friends and colleagues, Heiney was a long-time participant on the Community Hospital Board of Directors. He deepened his commitment to Community through his service on the Foundation's board of directors. Both he and his wife Betty cherished Community Hospital and had come to view service there as a cornerstone of their civic involvement and life as Indianapolis residents.

Heiney's background equipped him to leave a mark on the hospital. He'd grown up in Pennsylvania, met New York Yankees Babe Ruth and Lou Gehrig, and served in World War II under American General George S. Patton. Heiney's wartime experience with Patton included supervision of the building and operation of a large prisoner-of-war camp for German officers.

Moving to Indianapolis by the 1950s, Heiney had worked for almost twenty years as president of one of the city's most important organizations, the Indiana Gas Company, where C. Harvey Bradley, a member of both the gas company's board and Community Hospital's board, suggested Heiney join the board of the hospital. As had been true with Patton's army, with Indiana Gas Company, and with nearly every endeavor he undertook, Heiney demonstrated an unusual talent for new ideas, creative solutions, and openness to change. It was this talent that Allen Hicks tapped into during a conversation with Heiney in 1981.

In a private talk, Heiney and Hicks speculated about the future of both Indianapolis and Community Hospital. Heiney predicted that the city's next stage of population and economic growth would be in northeastern Marion County, likely in the vicinity of a small village known as Castleton. Castleton had been a stop on a railroad line, with large farms and a few houses clustered around the depot. Castleton was now flanked by Geist Reservoir, a main water source for Indianapolis. Home builders were just beginning to recognize the uniqueness of the lake in Marion County. Castleton was also near Interstate 465, a high-speed, four-lane highway that ran in an oval pattern within the edges of Marion County. In the mind of Jack Heiney, Castleton's barnyards and barbed-wire fences wouldn't exist for much longer, indeed they were already gone. For every barn, he saw new homes and shops. For every field and pasture, he saw businesses and parking lots. For every day on the calendar, he saw Castleton edging closer to the cusp of explosive change.

Because of his devotion to Community Hospital, Heiney met

with Hicks to discuss the relationship between the future of Marion County and the future of Community Hospital. To Heiney, the two things were joined. The hospital and the city—as embodied by the county—had to be considered together both in the present and in the future. This was where Heiney added a new layer to the kind of thinking that had given birth to Community Hospital in the first place. Back in the early 1950s, the growth of eastern Indianapolis and Marion County had happened around the hospital's founders. They envisioned Community fulfilling a burgeoning yet unmet need. For Heiney, though, the growth was not yet a reality. He was thinking in future time, of where current needs and trends were likely headed, and he wanted Hicks to think in the same way.

Heiney urged Hicks to think about the hospital's options five years, ten years, twenty years ahead. A geographic option was to think of Community as fixed, static, and far removed—the site of the hospital was several miles south of where Heiney expected massive growth to occur. Another option, however, could be more flexible, adaptive, and —with perhaps the hospital extending itself in a way it hadn't done before. This was strategic, not geographic.

Hicks agreed entirely with Heiney's visioning. The bond was powerful between the hospital and the places where the people of eastern Indianapolis and Marion County lived, worked, and raised families. He knew that. But the strongest bond stretches as well as holds, and since the 1950s it had stretched for Community Hospital to include new and innovative programs, services, capabilities, and responsibilities. Now the bond would stretch to include the choices and aspirations of where the hospital's patients and their descendants might live, in Castleton and perhaps other northern environs. Healthcare at Community Hospital began on Ritter Avenue. Hicks and Heiney wanted to ensure that it did not end there.

Hicks had similar conversations with his trusted vice president, Bob Clarke. Clarke lived in the vicinity of Castleton, one of the many new homes being built in the area. Clarke saw the potential of Castleton as he drove to and from the hospital every day. He asked his planning assistant, Kathy Norris, to look more closely at population estimates for the area. Clarke and Norris discovered that

82nd Street was expected to be an epicenter of growth. Clarke showed their findings to Hicks.

Hicks's inclination was to find a half-way point between Castleton and Community Hospital. He wondered if Fort Benjamin Harrison represented such a point. Fort Harrison was the site of a large military financial center along with some additional administrative and training operations. Hicks and Clarke began negotiations with federal officials. Talks dragged on month after month with no end in sight.

Hicks, Heiney, and Clarke agreed on the likelihood that other hospitals and healthcare organizations would come to the same conclusion about Castleton and the northern reaches of Indianapolis. Rumors had surfaced that Humana, which didn't yet have a hospital in Indianapolis, was mulling the possibility of building a women's hospital in northeastern Marion County. It wouldn't be long before other facilities might pop up in the farms and fields of the area. Hicks decided to abandon the Fort Harrison negotiations.

While the search for a location continued, a concurrent task was for Hicks and Heiney to build support within Community Hospital's board of trustees and their colleagues on the board of the Community Hospital Foundation. It was not easy. Over the course of several meetings, members of the two boards argued and debated the issue of Castleton expansion. The passion and intensity of exchanges among board members harkened back to the early 1960s when hospital board members had disagreed over the use of federal government funding for building expansion. As proved true then so it was again—the heated discussions reflected deeply-held convictions more than egos or personalities.

Two issues were the most controversial. First, many board members wanted the smallest parcel of acreage as a way to minimize the risk. Thirty acres seemed an acceptable amount. Hicks and Heiney, along with board chairperson John Hague of Naval Avionics, urged the group to go for a larger amount. Little by little they nudged the size upward in the meetings. The final allotment of 103 acres, which included acreage owned by Dr. Jean Mercho, represented as far as the entire board could be persuaded to go. The acreage was almost precisely on the spot first identified by Clarke and Norris in their first research and analysis.

The second issue was thornier than the first. Many board members worried that an additional site for healthcare would undermine Community's original facility and campus on Ritter Avenue. The new location, these members argued, would drain patient demand away from the hospital; no one could be sure that a patient seeking a test or treatment would leave to take advantage of the new closer location. The risk was high that Community was "cannibalizing" itself at a time of growing competition from other local healthcare providers.

The reduced-demand issue ran deeper than pure hospital economics. If existing patients were drawn off by a Castleton facility, some board members feared that medical staff and hospital personnel from Ritter Avenue would soon follow. And they would carry with them a further resource, invisible to the eye but holding immeasurable importance—the hospital's culture and, potentially, its identity. After all, it was Community's culture and identity that had made the hospital successful since the 1950s and had convinced Allen Hicks to become its second formal leader. Some board members feared a new property was just the first step to closing the hospital on Ritter Avenue.

The debate was fierce, the discussions intense. It was a replay of the internal board dynamics of the early 1960s when the issue was whether or not to accept federal government funding. Passions ran highest when purpose was at stake.

After lengthy wrangling, the boards cast their final votes. In addition to Hicks's urging for approval, such board members as John Hague, P.E. MacAllister, William Sigman, and Harry Gonso were active in persuading their colleagues to endorse the land purchase. As leaders in the community and respective professions, their word carried great weight. The decision to acquire the acreage in Castleton was also aided by the hospital's thin funding reserves and the consensus around a general plan to develop a health campus in northeastern Marion County. By fall 1981, the boards voted "yes" to spend $25 million for construction of a 100-bed hospital, an outpatient clinic, and a 125-bed psychiatric treatment center. Ambitiously, they set a 16-month schedule for completion. Hicks and Clarke negotiated feverishly with local real estate developer Howard Peterson on the financial arrangements. Hicks even ordered the bulldozers to begin work before the last details were complete.

The first phase of the construction began immediately with destruction of a barn and farmhouse. Within a short time at the Castleton property, only a grain silo was still standing from the original farm.

The silo symbolized a new era for Community Hospital. The facility on Ritter Avenue shared its name with other buildings on a separate campus. Like a cell subdividing itself, one hospital had become two. Unless circumstances compelled otherwise, the staff, employees, and patients at Community Hospital on Ritter Avenue would no longer exist without a companion facility on 82nd Street in Castleton. And thus, Community Hospital—the name understood to typify the hospital's unique bond between itself and the places people lived and worked—added a direction: Community Hospital East.

The new name belonged to a wave of changes rising up around Community Hospital East. These changes were of the sharpest sort. New entities sprouted up, including urgicenters (small medical facilities that provided basic care), surgicenters (routine surgical procedures in a day), health maintenance organizations (groups of healthcare payers and providers), and diagnostic-related groups (governmentally-priced categories of treatment). Beyond them, further pressures came from a severe under-supply of nurses, a glut of doctors and medical practices, efforts from competitors to recruit key staff away from Community East, and a dangerous shortage of available beds for patients.

The strain showed on Community Hospital by 1983. State government officials demanded further documentation on specific costs and expenses from the hospital. Officials from Community Hospital East testified to a committee in the Indiana state legislature that the burdens of complying with regulations and requirements were piling up on their staff. Separately, nurses and non-clinical staff alike warned that patients were expressing greater distress at their inability either to pay for medical costs or to understand the bizarrely complex environment of insurances companies, governmental agencies, and professional medical organizations. For the first time,

Community Hospital East hired a new vice president who would have responsibility for both the hospital on Ritter Avenue and for a multi-hospital partnership that involved Community. This new job position reflected new amoeba-like lines of organization and affiliation both within and without Community Hospital East.

The complexity of healthcare at Community Hospital East included the nature of treatment itself. Technology was becoming more prevalent at the hospital, intensifying the sense that fundamental changes were underway. Community Hospital East added a new laser device to treat patients who had suffered from cateracts, while Community's Hook Rehabilitative Center secured computers for patients to play video games—the technique improved recovery from brain injuries.

Computer technology enabled emergency room specialists to treat victims of a local workplace accident involving toxic vapors. New York-based computers reduced the time to identify the toxins and target a response at Community's facility on Ritter Avenue. Dr. Lance Trexler of Community Hospital East championed the potential use of drugs in accelerating recovery from brain damage. Trexler hosted a leading drug researcher at a six-day symposium held at the Indiana Convention Center. The rise of technology-driven medicine and the rise of healthcare costs seemed to point to a new era few people understood.

From the public's perspective, however, Community Hospital East was unchanging in its civic role of leadership. More than 200 local preschool children captured attention at the hospital with a visit to learn more about healthcare for their families. When asked why surgeons wore sterilized caps in the operating room, a young participant answered, "To keep germs off his head." This event, organized to celebrate Children's Hospital Week in 1983, symbolized the close connections between Community Hospital and families in the surrounding neighborhoods.

The people of Indianapolis saw new sides to Community Hospital East. The hospital allied with a locally popular broadcaster, Dick Wolfsie, to launch a television show highlighting health issues and treatments. Wolfsie's style was a combination of the latest medical information and folksy informality, making him a perfect fit as a television intermediary between the hospital and the public. Community's public relations director, Patricia Mosier, also hit upon the idea of using a popular television comedy show to widen interest in a local blood drive. Mosier and a team of Community nurses and staff adopted costumes and characters from the show "MASH", a nationally popular comedy series depicting scenes from the Korean War. Mosier's efforts resulted in one of the highest amount of donations for a blood drive in Indianapolis.

Community Hospital East's ongoing imprint on Indianapolis was still highly visible. Hospital executive Allen Hicks was invited to join a small group of Indianapolis leaders to help design a new economic development strategy for the city. Hicks was part of an exclusive effort to fund and launch a new economic development organization meant to boost business and industry in Indianapolis. Having assisted in bringing the headquarters of Kiwanis International to Indianapolis, Hicks had a rich pool of experience to draw from in guiding the city's new economic development entity.

Hicks's influence ranged far beyond Ritter Avenue. He had an extraordinary record of developing young leaders, particularly aspiring hospital executives who served with him as administrative interns. Youthful leaders like Mark Moore and Steve Reed watched Hicks closely and sought to emulate his practices later in their careers. "He was the consummate CEO for a great number of us young administrative interns," said Doug Deck. "Our success as CEOs in large teaching hospitals and systems was because of him," Deck stated.

One of Hicks's lessons could be clearly seen in the internal culture of the hospital on Ritter Avenue. The culture was an important reason behind Community Hospital East's endurance in the face of change. Despite rumors that a potential closure of the hospital had to be at the root of the Castleton expansion, the culture of the medical staff, clinical personnel, and non-clinical workforce held fast to its identity. The after-work socializing and special family-oriented events that had emerged at Community over the past fifteen years fueled resilience and steadfastness among caregivers. Mutual support helped to calm fears.

The strength of the hospital's culture was also seen in the Women's Auxiliary. Heedless of the changes lashing at Community Hospital

East, the Women's Auxiliary stood firm as a pillar of continuity. The group raised money to buy the latest technology for baby crib monitors and operated the telephone help line for local elderly men and women. Mrs. Russell Schulz led a group of volunteers to raise money to purchase new-born infant warmers.

The Auxiliary continued to inspire thousands of hours of activity, with Mrs. George Romy, Mrs. Goodwin Danner, Mrs. Churchill Wilson, Mrs. Frank Felkins, and Mrs. Ralph Goulet each receiving honors for more than 8,000 hours of service at the hospital. The volunteers who worked at Community Hospital East on Ritter Avenue were a steadying influence on the hospital, a constantly flowing source of its culture and identity.

The year 1983 closed with a trio of events that illustrated the world confronting Community Hospital's original campus on Ritter Avenue. The people of Indianapolis suffered through the worst cold weather in more than a century, with temperatures plunging far below zero. Residents from eastern Marion County and the east-side of Indianapolis turned to Community Hospital for treatment and relief from severe frost bite and exposure as well as a temporary source of heat and warm food. Community Hospital's telephone help line was crucial in assisting local elderly residents whose furnaces had broken down. Five years after the city's worst blizzard, Community Hospital served again as a neighborhood outpost in a winter crisis.

The bitter winter was the perfect setting for Community Hospital to celebrate the work of one of its most popular volunteers, the aptly-named Frost Swisher. Swisher was ninety-two years old, and his story appeared in Indianapolis's most popular newspaper, where readers learned about his unique bond to Community Hospital.

Since the early 1970s, Swisher had been greeting and welcoming patients as they entered Community Hospital from Ritter Avenue, a fixture at the front door. Everyone at Community Hospital—patients, doctors, nurses, staff, executives—knew Swisher for his warm hello, friendly manner, and willingness to spend time with people he thought needed an extra smile. He often ate at the hospital cafeteria, lunches and dinners alike, where he said the food "was as good as anywhere in town."

Swisher's history was like Community's history. He had grown with the city. Swisher had been a mechanic at the Indianapolis Motor Speedway back when the racetrack had first opened, in the 1910s. A racecar mechanic in those days rode with the driver, which Swisher had done at the Speedway. A few years later Swisher left his job repairing racecars and opened his own business, transporting milk in trucks from farms to retailers. He'd sold his company. His wife Flossie had been a professional model at L.S. Ayres stores, one of the most recognizable stores in Indianapolis. She had quit her job after she was asked to model underwear. With no children and moving into a life of retirement, Frost and Flossie Swisher had devoted themselves to various causes in Indianapolis. Community Hospital East had been at the top of their list.

With the death of his wife, Frost Swisher had found increasing comfort in volunteering at Community Hospital East. His time at Community softened his loss. "The past is for memories," Swisher told a newspaper reporter, "today is for living." So it was. The conversations that vanished at home were the chats he still had at Community. The companionship not available after his wife's passing were the relationships he cherished with staff and co-volunteers at Community. The service no longer offered to his racecar drivers and milk-truck customers was the attention he gave to patients and their families at Community. Rising above the changes in the life of one man as well as eastern Indianapolis and Marion County, Frost Swisher and Community Hospital embraced every man, woman, and child through the front door off Ritter Avenue.

Nearing the year's end, another winter storm had come and gone, another crisis had brought the neighborhood into the sheltering arms of Community Hospital. Nearing a life's end, another volunteer expressed a heart-felt connection to Community Hospital and the people who gave or received care in its healing environment. And now nearing a tenure's end, in the last of the trio of symbolic moments, Allen Hicks mulled in his mind whether or not it was time for a change. To make that change a reality for both himself and for Community Hospital East, he had to make a phone call. Around the moments of the frigid winter storm and Frost Swisher's newspaper article, Allen Hicks picked up his telephone and dialed the number of a friend.

CHAPTER 9
New Sheriff In Town, 1984-1991

At his home in western Pennsylvania, a 41-year old man picked up his telephone and heard the voice of Allen Hicks, his friend from Indianapolis. Hicks spoke to him for several minutes. The man listened to Hicks, thanked him for calling, and hung up the phone. A look of thoughtfulness, of introspection, covered his face.

Such was the method of leadership succession at Community Hospital East.

The 41-year old man was William Corley. A native of a small town near Pittsburgh, Corley had known Hicks for many months. Corley regarded Hicks as one of the ten best hospital leaders in the United States. For his part, Hicks believed that Corley was his natural replacement, the only one who could continue to build upon the legacy of Community Hospital East and the emerging larger entity that spanned two facilities. Hicks had urged, urged to the point of demanding in the nicest way possible, that Corley actively seek to succeed him.

William Corley came from a solid family background. His father worked as a labor negotiator and vice president of a large company, his mother as a substitute teacher. As the middle child in a three-son family, he loved sports as a youth and earned a football scholarship at The College of William & Mary. Among his coaches at William & Mary was future Notre Dame football coaching legend, Lou Holtz.

One of the most formative parts of Corley's background was military service. Corley had served in the Reserve Officer Training Corps (ROTC) at The College of William and Mary. Having developed an interest in the financial aspects of healthcare while in graduate school at Duke University, he moved on to Walter Reed Military Hospital in Washington DC, serving as administrator for the Armed Forces Institute of Pathology. From there Corley had volunteered to finish his two-year ROTC commitment in Vietnam. He was stationed at the Third Army Hospital in Saigon, South Vietnam in the late 1960s, serving at the pivotal point when anti-war sentiment at home began to burn its hottest. These military experiences allowed Corley to build upon a natural preference for discipline, organization, and competitiveness. With his close-cropped haircut and a ramrod-straight manner of walking, Corley exuded the habits of a former soldier.

Corley followed his military service with healthcare work on an administrative level. He held top-shelf positions at a major consulting firm, the University of Kentucky Medical Center, Hershey Medical Center in Hershey, Pennsylvania, and Akron General Medical Center in northeastern Ohio. At each stop along the way Corley strengthened his knowledge of the latest management techniques, organizational theory, and healthcare innovations. Many of his most cherished professional relationships were with those who, like him, excelled at the analysis and improvement of processes and structures that comprised healthcare. Corley enjoyed working on the most innovative design features of healthcare organizations and services.

Corley revered Allen Hicks. To him, Hicks was one of the most influential hospital leaders in the nation. He applauded the way in which Hicks pushed ahead on entrepreneurial strategies and projects. It was a quality often lacking in many healthcare organizations. Corley admired Hicks not only for his bold leadership but also for his personal style. He viewed Hicks as a leader at ease on the move; he praised Hicks for building connections to other leaders of high stature and broad prestige. With a degree of self-awareness lacking in some leaders, Corley admitted that he didn't have Hicks's ability to charm and embrace.

In fact, Corley believed it was this lack of Hicks's personable manner that would prevent him from becoming the new chief executive officer at Community Hospital. When he met with board members of both the hospital and Foundation, Corley made a point of emphasizing his preference for "staying in the office and in the building" rather than traveling to national meetings and conferences. The sharp turn from Hicks's style would, in Corley's opinion, shut the door on his potential succession of Hicks at Community Hospital East.

Corley hadn't reckoned with either Hicks or the respective boards of Community. For one thing, many board members, including Indiana Central College (University of Indianapolis) President Gene Sease, took an instant liking to Corley. For another, Hicks used his powers of persuasion and also his influence with the boards of the hospital and the Foundation that he had stockpiled over the years. He urged them to look beyond any differences in style that separated he and Corley and to probe more into the core of things. Corley himself struck upon a magnetic theme: he wanted to keep and expand the spirit of innovation at Community. His assertion impressed the boards with a powerful understanding of the forces at work in healthcare in Indianapolis, the Midwest, and nationwide. His bearing—that military-oriented bearing embodied in the conservative suit and wing-tip shoes he wore to the interview—struck them as serious and determined. To a person, board members believed Corley was precisely the leader they needed.

The boards accepted Hicks's recommendation on Corley. They offered the position to William Corley by the start of 1984 and he accepted.

The organization he inherited was robust. Community Hospital East encompassed Hook's Rehabilitation Center, Gallahue Mental Health Center, Pain Rehabilitation Center, Wright Institute of Otology, Regional Cancer Center, Center for Sports Medicine, a cardiac rehabilitation program, an intensive care nursery, and a full array of emergency medicine services.

Corley's first day at Community Hospital East was a shock to him. The chairperson of the hospital board, Boris Meditch, president of National Wholesale Grocery Company, met Corley in his office at the hospital. Amiable, friendly, and welcoming, Meditch casually asked Corley if he'd like an introduction to a few people. Corley said yes and thanked Meditch. Meditch picked up Corley's telephone, dialed two phone numbers, and within five minutes both he and Corley were on that morning's schedules, respectively, of the governor of Indiana and the mayor of Indianapolis. Meditch told Corley to get his coat. Amazed, Corley followed Meditch for his first two meetings in downtown Indianapolis beyond Community Hospital East. Later on, Corley called his former secretary back at Akron, Ohio. "It's not at all like my old job," he said. The first day signaled things to come.

William Corley was now the third formal leader of the original Community Hospital and of the two-facility organization that spanned Ritter Avenue and Castleton. Corley entered a situation vastly different from that confronted by his predecessors W.C. McLin and Allen Hicks. The trick would be for Corley to perceive and act on the real nature of the difference.

The contrast in the styles of Hicks and Corley had pleased the boards, but it wasn't at all certain it would fit well with the culture of Community Hospital East. Hicks was evangelical and gregarious with doctors, nurses, staff, patients, and patients' families. They accepted and liked his style. Corley's manner appeared quite different, and reactions from within the hospital—a place where Corley told the boards he would spend nearly all of his time—were decidedly unknown. In terms of Corley's success or failure as successor to Hicks, his acceptance or rejection by the people who made the hospital's culture would be key.

A potential issue was that Corley's style was easy to misread. With his deep voice, serious demeanor, and orderly appearance, people might have concluded too quickly that he was rigid and exacting in his use of authority. They might also feel intimidated by him. No one would have been shocked to learn Corley had a military background.

Corley decided the best approach was to be himself. The worst thing would be for Corley to become caught up in the whirlwind of his new position and seek to act like someone he was not. Rather than imitate Hicks, Corley relied on his innate humility, quietness, and modesty.

Corley conceived of a few leadership techniques that would stay with him for as long as he was with Community. He developed a strong, trusting relationship with his executive assistant; the two of them began an annual practice of sharing a list of five prioritized expectations that each had of the other.

Also, Corley enjoyed jogging. He started a habit of entering organized charity runs on the weekends. He invited Community employees and their spouses to run with him. If they bested him in the race, Corley met each of his running companions and worked in their departments for an hour in the weeks after the run. They also had an open invitation to meet again with Corley whenever necessary. Corley's assistant kept a list of these participants so that Corley could check on their views of how the hospital was functioning. In addition, Corley started walking around the hospital at frequent intervals. Using a then-popular tool of "management-by-walking-around," Corley conducted brief, informal chats with staff throughout the hospital. The chats had a specific purpose, with Corley gleaning topics he could later formulate into questions for his vice presidents. Corley also continued Allen Hicks's "round-table talks" where employees would chat with the hospital's formal leader in small groups.

Corley added basketball to his list of activities that connected him to employees. Steve Boyd, a technician popular for his easy manner and reliable work ethic, developed a fondness for playing basketball and CHE physicians and staff. Boyd credited the regularity of eight-hour shifts with giving him and other CHE employees the time to shoot baskets with Corley. In later years, twelve-hour shifts would exhaust employees, leaving them with only the desire to return home after a long stint at the hospital.

Through these methods, Corley developed a vast network of contacts and information across Community Hospital East as well as other Community facilities. One employee joked that it was "a version of the Central Intelligence Agency" that helped Corley keep informed about attitudes, trends, and issues at Community. Like all good humor, the joke touched on a deeper truth—unlike Hicks, whose relationships resembled that of a preacher to his flock, Corley preferred interactions built around shared interests and common goals. The network was a perfect expression of Corley's original decision to be himself and through his natural style gain access to vast amounts of information.

It wasn't long before Corley had crystallized his own vision for Community Hospital East and other facilities. The vision had a thread: exceptionalism. Corley sought exceptional patient experience, exceptional employee experience, and exceptional doctors' experience. Corley believed that if Community acted on all three forms of exceptionalism, then financial benefits would follow. The hospital's vision, values, and culture preceded finances. CHE's pursuit of exceptionalism found expression in a marketing phrase—"The Community Commitment. To Your Health."

Corley's vision of exceptionalism would build upon the culture of Community Hospital East. The culture was at a unique stage. For the first time in the life of the hospital, the internal culture, its way of being—the relationships, habits, attitudes, and traits of people as they worked together over time—would exist not in and of itself, but alongside that of the new hospital in Castleton.

William Corley entered the world of Community Hospital East at precisely the moment when the people there were both acutely aware of themselves as a group and nervous about their status in an expanded organization. Corley soon perceived that the exceptionalism of Community Hospital East had to be broadened to include Community Hospital North and any other new or existing facilities that would be added to the group or, as Corley termed it, the "System." And simultaneously, Community's culture would need to cope with a changing world of healthcare that Dr. Glenn Bingle, medical education director, predicted would soon rely on the elderly for the bulk of inpatient cases. It was change upon change upon change. The culture of Community Hospital East would feel a great strain under this weight.

Compared to Corley, a new nurse on one of the floors of the Twin Towers had a head-start on knowing the culture. Married to Glenn Bingle, Jan Bingle was a nurse who had started working at the hospital not long before Corley's arrival. Both Glenn and Jan Bingle talked often about the hospital, whether at home or at work, and they agreed that Community Hospital East was like an "organism," an organization with heart, soul, bone, and muscle. Jan Bingle explained that "everyone had extended family who worked there, who had been patients there, and who were learning about their careers and professions there." Family, health, and education, all under one roof, Bingle's observation showed that for many people, Community Hospital East functioned as a home away from home. William Corley represented the stranger standing at the home's front door.

"Home" suggested other cultural images for Community Hospital East. Deb Smith, a colleague of the Bingles who worked in the hospital's credit deparment, had grown up within walking distance of the facility on Ritter Avenue and had toured the building when it had first opened in 1956. By the mid-1980s she was a long-time employee. From a girl of childhood to a woman of adulthood, she had lived her entire life thus far within sight of Community Hospital East. She estimated that by the time of Corley's hiring the typical nurse had worked there for nearly twenty years and that patients often remained in the hospital for as long as three weeks. These lengths of time— almost two decades for staff and a half-month for patients—produced a rich texture of relationships at the hospital. It was, Smith concluded, the feeling of "a close-knit family."

Many in Community traveled a unique path from family to patient to employee. Nurse Tonya Longwell was among them. She so embraced the culture that she envisioned spending her career at Community Hospital East. Connie Thompson was born at Community and her mother worked there as a nurse. Thompson found her first meaningful job at Community, spent part of her wedding night in the emergency room when her husband suffered a motorcycle accident, and gave birth to three of their children at Community, one of whom would later work at the hospital. The same multi-generational story was true for Anjanette Wicker, whose parents and siblings, followed by her own family, had used the hospital. When she became a nursing student in college, Wicker made Community into her workplace of choice and never looked back. Cheryl Mosley joined the pharmacy at Community immediately after graduating from high school, rising eventually to positions that spanned the entire Community system. Her eldest daughter crossed the hospital's generational bridge and became a nurse at Community. Jill Turner worked at Community and also welcomed one of her children to the hospital for employment. Kathy Stroud began at Community as a student volunteer, then an adult volunteer, and finally became a licensed practical nurse at the hospital. Mary Conway grew up in the local neighborhood, was a student volunteer and then obtained her nursing degree in her 30s, after which she worked for years in various departments. Later, she became a patient at Community—"I owe them my life," she said, "Community is my home...part of my DNA." Martha Commodore relished Community's eastside culture, describing her team, the radiology department, as a "second family" in her life for having "always shown compassion." Dr. Mark Knopp was born at Community, had his childhood illnesses and injuries treated at the hospital, and made lifelong friendships while a resident there. "I liked the character of Community and the relationships," he said.

The family took care of itself. Karri Amory, a radiologist, said that "everyone helped everyone" and many staff also spent time together away from work, another reason "it always felt like a family." Deb Smith explained that because everyone knew each other so well they were willing to give money to impoverished patients who might not be able to buy food after leaving the hospital, and often agreed to visit discharged patients in their homes to check on their condition. This family-style culture of caregiving, Smith said, "was just how it was."

The warmth of Community's family feeling took on surprising forms. Chief operating officer Charlie Evans was the beneficiary of a campaign to celebrate his fortieth birthday in unforgettable fashion. When not at work, Evans loved to sing. Departments at Community banded together and arranged for Evans to sing the National Anthem at a Cincinnati Reds baseball game. More than 600 Community employees traveled to Cincinnati to witness Evans's talents on that special August night in 1987.

The vital role of physicians at CHE also helped with the hospital's family atmosphere. Widely respected and deeply knowledgeable, Dr. William McGarvey was generous with his time as he cultivated relationships among clincial and support staff alike. He always greeted the telephone operators, smiled and chatted with nurses and technicians, and ensured that his patients felt completely at home in the facility. In a profession sometimes known for aloofness and intimidation, McGarvey embodied a warmth and friendliness that defined the physicians at CHE.

Bruce Hopkins was another familiar physician at CHE. He had worked with the hospital since the 1960s. He was skilled in emergency medicine and in the specialty of ear-nose-throat cases. He had left California to come to CHE because it "was the place I wanted to work." Hopkins and other doctors talked constantly about Indiana University basketball. He regarded the process of surgery at CHE as the best in Indianapolis and was particularly proud of the high quality of nursing. Hopkins was known as an exhaustive worker in surgery and was selfless in accepting the most difficult cases. Doctors such as McGarvey and Hopkins set a lofty standard for CHE's physicians.

Lou Bojrab and Larry Monn were other doctors at this time. They were dedicated, energetic, and passionate about providing unsurpassed health care to their patients. They helped make the emergency department one of the best in Indiana. Bojrab compared the warm feeling among hospital staff to "going to your grandparents for Thanksgiving." He was especially proud of the care offered to the indigent; he sang "performing for Jesus" softly to himself while he worked on these cases. They saw a colleague, Dr. Herschel Moss perform surgery without charging any fees to impoverished patients. Moss would often fly a small plane to Batesville, Indiana and do the same thing there. Monn secured a loan from a local bank to pay for his surgical equipment, a practice replicated by many CHE doctors. Both Monn and Bojrab attested to the prevalent attitude among their peers that they were delivering an almost sacred service rather than participating in a profession. The sense of a family sacrificing for others was everywhere.

Young doctors such as Doug Kuhn were newly arriving on the scene and added to the powerful closeness of the staff. Kuhn was the grandson of George A. Kuhn, Sr, an original board member and the first honorary board director at Community Hospital East. Part of a generational stream flowing through the hospital, young Kuhn embodied the sense of duty and commitment passed on from family member to family member at the hospital. The orthopedic practice that

Kuhn launched was more than continued tradition. It was a living, working monument to the hospital's family roots.

Left on its own, however, CHE's feeling of family had a potential problem. This attitude might easily have sunk into an "us-versus-them" mentality, excluding outsiders and newcomers, Corley among them. However, the good news for Corley was that the culture of Community Hospital East was a source of inspiration rather than insulation, of inclusion rather than exclusion. Smith asserted that among doctors, nurses, and staff—Mary Ita Moriarty, Anne Schafer, Darlene Seals, Dorothy Copeland, the list of deeply devoted employees on Ritter Avenue went on and on—people at the organization "were always ready to go above and beyond the call of duty."

At roughly the same time as Corley, another young man arrived at CHE. He was Bryan Mills, a 24-year old accountant not long out of college and in his just his second professional job. He was one of three new accountants at the hospital. He was tasked with the daunting challenge of developing a financial system and methodology for CHE which, incredibly, had lacked one until now. Mills had to make financial sense out of financial senselessness.

Mills plunged into his work. Seated in a metal chair behind a folding card table, Mills poured over every document he could find with a dollar sign on it. After consuming these stacks of paper, Mills turned to an unlikely place for a young accountant—he began to talk to everyone about all aspects of daily operations at Ritter Avenue. He came to know nearly the entire workforce as well as each nook and cranny of the place. In the founding moment of his professional life, he immersed himself in Community Hospital East. Accomplishing his task of framing a financial system at the hospital, Mills's self-education would serve as an excellent foundation for his subsequent career at Community. He would rightly earn the label "entrepreneur extraordinaire."

The hospital's culture that Mills observed was a good fit for Corley's vision of exceptionalism. The rest of the 1980s and early 1990s revealed the tight connection between vision and culture. Newly hired project manager Terry Northern helped organize a special 30-year anniversary event, complete with a picnic, family games, and food served under large tents.

Doctors and staff at CHE achieved important successes. Dr. Richard Eaton developed a bone bank at the hospital. Pieces of bone were frozen and stored until needed in replacement surgery. Dr. Jean Mercho provided vital expertise in creating a cardiovascular program at Union Hospital in Terre Haute. Dr. Francis Price Jr was among the first in Indiana to use a new drug, Human Epidermal Growth Factor, to improve the rate of patient recovery after corneal transplants. Dr. Ray Scott Jr offered the latest surgical techniques in balloon insertions for the purpose of weight loss. Doctors in the emergency department began to analyze burn treatment strategies by employing computer printouts via transmission from specialists located in New York. The computer-based program enabled Community doctors to help treat victims of an accident at an engineering company not far from Ritter Avenue. A new world of medicine was unfolding at CHE.

It was a doctor, Larry Monn, who gave a stirring speech at a large CHE function held at the Marriott Inn, just a short distance away from the hospital. Monn told the crowd of executives, departmental directors, and numerous managers that the future of the hospital depended on its ability to maintain unity within the organization. Monn appealed to the history of Community as well as to the sense of duty and mission shared by the people in attendance. Monn's words were so impactful that Bryan Mills could recall their power more than thirty years later.

Monn's unity speech flowed from a hospital that was attracting major awards. Dr. Scott Green was one of only twenty recipients in the US to obtain a Mead-Johnson Award for scholarship and leadership in family medicine. Dr. Steven Isenberg became Physician of the Year for the Family Practice Residency Program. Dr. Floyd Boyer, a retired physician at Community, was one of eight doctors chosen by his peers to enter the Fellowship of Distinguished Physicians. Betty Hogsett won Nurse of the Year honors. A professional media award went to the hospital for its annual conference, "From A Woman's Point of View."

The vision and culture of exceptionalism were clear in CHE's impact on Indianapolis and central Indiana. Sue Heffron, a nurse, led a multi-disciplinary team to design and implement the "Parent Support Committee" to help parents cope with stillborn infants. David Llewellyn created "Picture This", a mental health initiative that used theater and drama to assist people struggling with AIDS, depression, attempted suicide, and more. The Regional Cancer Center received letters of thanks along with financial donations from patients and their families. Similar praise was directed at the new Chest Pain Unit, described by one patient as "a great addition to our community." A new CHE "Same Day Surgery Center" was one of the most noteworthy additions in Indianapolis. No other facility in the metropolitan area offered a similar scale of services, amenities, and quick-moving medical treatment.

The efforts of CHE appeared throughout the region. Nurse Janet McCutchan was the hospital-wide coordinator for CHE's involvement in the Pan American Games hosted in the city in 1987; clinical and support staff alike learned Spanish for international guests visiting for the event. Another nurse, Julie Painter, was regional chairperson of National Cancer Survivors Day in 1989. Debbie Price and a nurses' team trained local restaurant workers on helping people who choked on food. Doctors and nurses from CHE were prominent in a city-wide skin cancer screening program.

The emergency medical staff was especially active in the community. They participated at Fort Benjamin Harrison in training simulation sessions for local disaster response. Alternative Health Delivery director Jaquie Johnson organized another team from emergency medicine to provide as-needed treatment and services for crowds attending events at the newly built Hoosier Dome in downtown Indianapolis.

Some of CHE's civic contributions extended beyond healthcare. Bill Corley and one of his vice presidents, Anita Harden, donated part of their time to Indiana's state government. Corley and Harden reviewed the effectiveness of the state's program in health and human services. For their efforts they earned commendations as "Sagamores of the Wabash" by Governor Evan Bayh. Moreover, Corley volunteered to conduct training in quality-control principles to officials at the Indianapolis Public School system. Nurse Teresa Dickerson garnered public attention when she was sent to a medical facility in Washington state. Dickerson's temporary transfer enabled US Naval Reserve personnel to leave the Washington hospital and join US military forces preparing to liberate Kuwait in the Persian Gulf War.

In small ways and large, the people of greater Indianapolis responded with gratitude. The Women's Auxiliary was a fixture in the channeling of community support. Annual social events attracted financial support for renovations of the pediatrics unit, the Hooks Rehabilitation Center, and the Regional Cancer Center.

In addition, the region's residents applauded CHE through other means. Indianapolis Colts quarterback Jeff George paid a visit to the hospital to lift the spirits of 17-year old Andy Chalfant. Indianapolis Mayor William Hudnut expressed his appreciation for the excellent care he received after ankle surgery. Cory Elliott, a severe burn victim from Gary, Indiana, praised the skill and encouragement he found at Hook Rehabilitation Center. And the parents of their 20-year old son, who had died from acute lymphotic leukemia, wrote a heartfelt letter of gratitude to the Indianapolis Star, citing the heroic service of Jenney Polley, Susan Knapp, Dorothy Clark, Julie Painter, Jackie Maurice, and Dr. Shivaji Gunale. Their first Christmas without their son, the parents wrote, would be slightly easier for the tremendous compassion shown at CHE. From around Indiana, people offered thanks for the care given at CHE.

With all of CHE's positive work in the region, Bill Corley still needed to monitor closely the financial health of the hospital. In 1985 chief financial officer Ted Milkey announced that Community would help people deal with rising costs through a discount program. Patients who paid their bill within a month received a discount in the hospital's fees. A gambler by hobby who also played in professional blackjack tournaments in Las Vegan, Milkey used all his creative skills to keep the hospital solvent, including transferring pension funds from local banks to Wall Street to get higher returns. Separately, Corley decided to launch Pro Health Network after a payment dispute with Blue Cross Blue Shield. CHE also joined VHA Tri State to strengthen its economic position. Corley became president of United Health Services in a local effort to enhance collective purchasing power among central Indiana hospitals.

In summer 1991 the unveiling of the two-year building and renovation project brought William Corley's first phase of leadership at CHE to a close. A new main entrance greeted people arriving at the hospital. A drop-off area enhanced the ease with which drivers could pull their vehicles alongside the front doors and then move toward a 1300-car parking garage. The lobby opened up to an information desk, gift shop, and comfortable seating area. Hallways led off toward the Twin Towers and other parts of the hospital. Doctors, medical specialists, and their respective administrative staffs occupied a new professional building adjacent to the hospital. A refreshed feeling flowed from the completed project.

The project to expand and upgrade the hospital had the surprising effect of deepening relationships among CHE's workforce. With asphalt torn up, employees had been compelled to park in remote lots and board busses for a short ride into work. During the rides, employees passed the time with conversation. Some of them struck up romances that led to marriages. No one had foreseen this unintended yet happy consequence.

Corley demonstrated that he understood the hospital's culture. He did so by continuing the founding ceremony of 1955 and the Twin Towers of 1964 when he decided to bury another time capsule during the expansion opening of 1991. Staff and volunteers from CHE selected items important to them at this moment—newspapers detailing the Gulf War of 1990-1991; printed materials on quality improvement (a favorite topic of Corley's); a video of a television commercial about Community, among other things. The act of filling and burying the capsule symbolized one of the organization's enduring traditions.

The excitement of the expansion reached into every corner of the hospital. For the first time in anyone's memory, CHE staff contacted one of the largest newspapers in Indianapolis to announce the winner of hospital's "I Made A Difference" award. The winner was Daniel Pritt, who had worked for ten years at CHE. Pritt was praised as someone who "really cares about what he does, understands its importance, and always strives to please his customers." Pritt's "enthusiastic, helpful attitude" affected those around him." Regardless of the surroundings, "he always has a smile on his face."

The most surprising part of the award was that Pritt wasn't a doctor, nurse, paramedic, or health technician. He copied paper, the operator of the hospital's copy center. Pritt's honor reflected the broader meaning of the hospital's finished building project. On Ritter Avenue everyone's job was important, from the folks who helped patients through the new front door to the man who handled paper in the copy center, everyone lent a hand in CHE's unmatched patient care.

With lifted spirits and raised morale, Community Hospital East had a promising start to the final decade of the 20th century. That was fortunate, because a series of troubling changes waited just over the horizon.

CHAPTER 10
The Gathering Clouds, 1991-2004

Before dawn of any day in the early 1990s, a glance out the windows of Community Hospital's Twin Towers brought the same view it always did. In the last moments of night, from this, one of the highest spots in eastern Indianapolis, you saw the neighborhoods, across the trees and along the rooftops. Homes, businesses, factories, and churches were dimly visible. The lights of a car or truck moved along a street. Slowly, the eastern sky brightened, the darkness retreated, and the morning horizon of Ritter Avenue emerged unchanged.

This look was deceiving. Farther out, clouds were gathering and as they did the questions gathered, too. Was a storm in the making? And if a storm came, would it damage CHE?

The answers were not clear.

The first clouds came from the east, from William Corley's home state of Pennsylvania. In 1991, a special election had been held in Pennsylvania following the death of US Senator John Heinz. The campaign to succeed Heinz received national attention as a bellweather event for the next year's presidential election. The Democratic Party, in particular, spent massive amounts of money on the contest, and major television networks reported frequently on the candidates. The winning candidate in the Pennsylvania election was Harris Wofford, a Democrat.

Wofford won the election in large part because of his position on health care. Wofford emphasized the heavy load of health care costs and the struggles of many middle-class American families in carrying this burden. Wofford depicted health care as a survival-of-the-fittest battle between greedy insurers, doctors, and hospitals on one side and helpless patients and families on the other. The remedy, Wofford stated, was a more rational, efficient, and effective "system." Wofford's victory in the Pennsylvania election was interpreted by political observers as proof that American voters wanted "real change in health care."

The attitudes revealed by Wofford's victory were stirring at CHE. Through actions taken by CEO William Corley and CFO Ted Milkey, Community Hospital East participated in a "preferred provider organization", or PPO, a network comprised of hospitals and doctors. The PPO to which Community belonged provided services at prices designed to attract and hold patients to the network. Echoing words used by Wofford in Pennsylvania, Corley stated in early 1992, "Our patients and payers are saying to us...'health care costs are too high.'"

Wofford's campaign and victory caught the attention of political observers around the nation. Among them was a young, ambitious, intelligent, and fast-thinking Democrat in Arkansas, Governor Bill Clinton. Clinton embraced the label of "change in health care" and quickly climbed into the frontrunner's position as the Democratic nominee for president in 1992. Along with his wife Hillary, Bill Clinton toured the nation in 1992 and sought votes as a "new Democrat" who would overhaul health care if elected president. Clinton won the 1992 Democratic nomination and went on to defeat incumbent president George H.W. Bush to become President of the United States. A few months later in his first State of the Union speech, President Bill Clinton declared, "Later this spring (1993), I will deliver to Congress a comprehensive plan for health care reform that will finally get costs under control." A powerful government-based change seemed destined to strike health care. Community's William Corley likened it to a "medical arms race."

But one cloud isn't a storm. Similarly, in the early 1990s, CHE wasn't threatened solely by the rise of a large if unknown form of governmental power and reform. No, the greater concern arose from the presence of another cloud that would surely blend with the first and which together, portended a substantial risk to the very existence of the hospital on Ritter Avenue.

Indeed, the other cloud was Ritter Avenue itself.

Despite a generally rising national and state economy in 1992-1993, much of which was driven by computers and information technology, the east side of Indianapolis was in the midst of economic decline. CHE sat in the middle of factories and manufacturing plants that were either slumping in productivity and profitability or simply closing altogether. Over more than a decade, thousands of men and women had lost their jobs at International Harvestor, Western Electric, Chrysler, Navistar, and Ford. Many of these workforces were unionized; employees had earned significantly higher wages than in comparable companies elsewhere. The loss of these higher incomes hit local tax revenues especially hard. The jobs were gone and they weren't coming back.

Compounding the private sector job losses were cutbacks in government employment in eastern Indianapolis. Employment shrank at Naval Avionics and Fort Harrison Financial Center. As with the factories, workers at these government installations had earned substantial wages and salaries. Now they too were gone.

The shock of the economic blast spread across the east side. Retail shopping faltered at such local sites as Washington Square and Eastgate Malls. Smaller companies that provided services to the faltering larger employers suffered sharp drops in profits. They announced worker lay-offs of their own. A steady loss of customers resulted in still more retail store closings. A destructive spiral had set in.

The people of eastern Indianapolis were the victims of the spiral. The number of young, upwardly mobile families slipped. Conversely, the rate increased for households led by the elderly on fixed incomes. Costs of living rose elsewhere in more affluent sections of Indianapolis, trapping the growing impoverished population where they were. With manufacturing jobs harder to find, unemployment rose, as did its accompanying social issues of crime, drugs, and family disunity. Fewer new companies were seeking to start up or relocate to the area. In the vicinity around CHE, the city government of Indianapolis spent more than $250,000 to refurbish apartments left empty by departing residents. Vacant buildings and lots multiplied.

Within CHE, the impact was felt most in obstetrics. Despite recording in 1993 the birth of the 100,000[th] baby born at the hospital, the number of new-born babies delivered at CHE had fallen off by nearly twenty percent in the last few years. Analysis at CHE showed a similar increase in births at suburban hospitals, especially in the fast-growing north and northeast side of Indianapolis. Community Hospital North had benefited from that growth. CHE had not.

The promised health care plan from the Clinton Administration didn't appear in spring 1993. The delay didn't prevent CHE from continuing to act on important internal changes. CEO William Corley kicked into high gear a quality improvement program called "Patient Care Pathways." The program sought to reduce costs in every corner of CHE. Patient Care Pathways received coverage in the local Indianapolis media. A patient, Raymond Ogle, described in a newspaper report his outstanding experience at CHE. He said it was far more efficient, integrated, and coordinated than any other time as a patient.

The genesis of Patient Care Pathways was keen observation of effective patient care techniques. Mary Ann Underhill, a key CHE leader in the effort, explained, "We wanted to see why some patients could go home in seven days and some patients were still here after ten days." The new quality improvement program experienced by Ogle and other CHE patients reflected the findings of Underhill and a team of doctors, nurses, and clinical staff. It was significant health care reform done on the hospital level.

In addition to Patient Care Pathways, CHE kept on its steady path of community involvement and excellent patient care while the national health care controversy raged on. A local Indianapolis comedian, Clara Trusty, shared in a newspaper her story of using humor to cope with her leukemia treatment at CHE. The Women's Auxiliary held clothing and plant sales to benefit specific units in the hospital. Caregivers such as Pamela Giles researched on best practices in nurses' roles in caring for diabetic patients. CHE employees banded together and collected items to help families in Skopje, Macedonia, the native home of Mother Teresa, who had received world-wide acclaim that year.

By late 1993 the Clinton health care plan was finally ready. Dubbed "HillaryCare" because First Lady Hillary Clinton had led the design effort, the plan called for massive restructuring and reorganization across the American landscape. Partisans on both sides argued over HillaryCare with television commercials, magazine and newspaper articles, talk radio chatter, speeches, and town hall meetings.

The Clinton health care plan smashed up against a groundswell of opposition. Momentum behind the plan began to stall in 1994. Clinton's Democratic Party suffered heavy losses in the 1994 congressional elections; a key reason was the unpopularity of HillaryCare. The Clinton Administration officially declared its efforts at an end the following year.

With the national health care debate dying out, the clouds on the horizon of Ritter Avenue seemed to have lifted. The horizon was clear.

Not quite.

As HillaryCare disappeared, different pressures on health care continued to gather. In Indianapolis, a new trend swept over the regional health care marketplace. The trend took its name from business and finance: "mergers and acquisitions."

The belief was that the bigger an organization, the stronger its position would be in a market and economy that punished inefficiency, slowness, and redundancies. To stave off these problems, two or more organizations would combine into a single, larger entity that would then slash costs and ramp up nimbleness. The new entity stood to have more resources with which to reach and maintain a competitive size.

This was more than theory. A similar wave of mergers and acquisitions had occurred elsewhere in the American economy. Many economists and business analysts judged that health care was one of the handful of industries not yet responsive to marketplace dynamics. Health care's turn in the barrel had come.

Community CEO William Corley was not alone in realizing the potential of mergers and acquisition in local health care. Executives, board members, and doctors at University, Methodist, St. Vincent, Riley, Wishard, and St. Francis Hospitals respectively were all thinking over the same issue for their organizations. In 1995 Methodist and University started talks on combining into a new health care provider. Local media reported on the move as one of the most important economic issues of the mid-1990s. The Robert Wood Johnson Foundation launched a research project into health care mergers and acquisitions in several American cities, including Indianapolis. A sort of merger mania gripped health care in greater Indianapolis.

Corley and a substantial number of Community's board members responded swiftly. They met with representatives from St. Vincent Hospital and established a process for identifying how the two hospitals could form into a single entity. A long series of meetings followed, with participants grappling over the mission, values, and resources of Community and St. Vincent. St. Vincent's contingent consisted of numerous consultants and technical experts. Community had a far smaller team made up of Corley and a few of his executives. Despite their exhaustive efforts, a deal couldn't be reached. Moreover, Community's board was deeply divided over the proposed merger. A slim majority voted to terminate the idea in August 1996. Corley revisited the concept of merger and acquisition two years later in discussions with St. Francis. Like before, a deal failed to materialize. There wasn't enough appetite for merger at Community.

The merger meetings occurred at a fateful time for Community Hospital East. In any connective relationship—whether multiple people or multiple organizations—stress finds the weakest points. Nerves were already frayed at CHE because of expansion at Community Health North and the ongoing decay of the eastern Indianapolis economy. People at CHE already worried openly about the possibility of closing the Ritter Avenue hospital. Staff and volunteers talked about closure in the inevitable "meetings-after-the-meetings", the moments when deeply-held views are shared in hallways, elevators, break areas, and lunch rooms. Corley heard these rumblings through his "CIA-like" network and paid serious attention to them. He decided to keep his office at CHE in order to signal his commitment to the founding hospital.

The merger talks with St. Vincent added to these fears. If any chance existed that Community North might be a cause for closure of CHE, then the pressure appeared that much greater to close CHE if St. Vincent—with a new central facility in northwest Indianapolis— had aligned with Community. If closure ever emerged as a topic in Community-St. Vincent discussions, the choice of potential withdrawal was an easy one between the high-growth northside or the no-growth east side. The weeks of meetings with St. Vincent had an unintended and yet perhaps unavoidable consequence of intensifying fears at CHE.

The fears also reflected a current attitude at CHE. The hospital on Ritter Avenue was still learning how to fit in a broader health care system known simply as "Community." "Community" now meant East, North, and South hospitals. System-wide executives made the final decisions on medical affairs, purchasing, and other departmental issues. Most of Community's health classes and public events were now rotated from hospital to hospital to hospital. The Foundation sold tickets at East, North, and South for its popular new fund-raising activity, the auctioning of a newly built home. Job advertisements in newspapers appeared under the title of Community with sub-categories of open positions at East, North, and South. The ads did include a quiet reference to CHE's legacy: anyone who attended hiring events would gather first at the CHE boardroom and then get information on jobs in all three Community facilities. The reference, though, was in smaller print, whispering a subtle uncertainty about CHE's organizational identity.

The rising Community Network also benefited Community Hospital East. In spring 1996 a new Community pediatric strategy rolled out at CHE. Trademarked as the "Family Way," both North and South hospitals had tested and adapted the new program for expectant mothers. The Family Way blended labor, delivery, recovery, and post-partum into one seamless offering of birth-focused services, available in the same room where mother and baby could stay together. CHE unveiled the program under a slightly modified name: the Family Room. The Family Room was a natural extension of the emphasis on family medicine at CHE.

A similar action recurred in 1999 with the opening of the Indiana

Surgery Center at CHE. Like the Family Room, CHE's version of the Indiana Surgery Center replicated previous work of the hospitals at North and South. And again like the Family Room's connection to the prestige of family medicine at CHE, the new Center flowed smoothly from the leadership tradition that doctors had consistently demonstrated since the founding of Community Hospital East.

The doctors at CHE helped blaze another trail for the Network in 1999. The dust was still settling on the controversies over HillaryCare when more major major governmental action—the 1997 Balanced Budget Act—entered the health care marketplace. The new law slashed funding for Medicare payments, especially hospitals that provided medical education to doctors. The law also compelled most hospitals to stop hiring doctors on their payrolls, a common technique for the past few years. Corley and the doctors at CHE collaborated on a new approach for aligning physicians with the hospital. By late 1999, they began the first primary care group practice in Indianapolis. The success of this effort built on a tradition of activist-doctors and physician-leadership rooted in Community's founding.

Through the challenges of economy, government, and an uncertain position within the new Community Network, CHE gained sustenance from its vibrant relationship with the surrounding community. People from Ritter Avenue and other neighborhoods were eager shoppers at the Women's Auxiliary "Pumpkins to Pointsetta" boutique of fall 1997, the proceeds of which went to CHE's cancer center. Mary Ann Olvey of the Indianapolis Obedience Training Club brought pets into the hospital for therapy on a weekly basis. Eleven companies from the vicinity of Ritter Avenue formed the Greater Indianapolis Employers Against Domestic Violence coalition in 1998 after a Community North employee was killed by her ex-husband. A Center of Hope program opened at CHE to train staff on responding to victims of rape and sexual assault. Fire fighters from Franklin, Indiana participated in training for life-saving techniques offered by CHE's emergency department. CHE employees helped local residents when Type O-Positive blood supplies ran low, a sudden onset of yellow-jacket bee stings afflicted nearby children, and staff from a Planned Parenthood facility were exposed to anthrax in a domestic terrorist attack.

Patients were also a source of resilience to the caregivers of CHE. Chick McGee, a local radio personality, expressed his gratitude to CHE for excellent care in double-bypass heart surgery. An elderly couple—aged 80 and 78 years, respectively—shared in a newspaper their story of a life spent together within sight of CHE. Shelby County Commmissioner Bruce Knecht praised hospital staff for his recovery after a drunk-driver nearly killed him in a car accident. A senior at Triton Central High School thanked CHE's caregivers for support in helping her graduate on time while still receiving cancer treatment. These expressions of gratitude revealed an enduring attitude of devotion to patients regardless of the circumstances swirling around the hospital.

Perhaps the greatest display of perseverance at CHE occurred in the hospital's worst controversy of the late 1990s. In 1999 a doctor was charged with pediatric malpractice. The doctor lashed out at CHE in retaliation. A formal investigation ensued, with CHE's pediatric nurses displaying courage and resolve in public testimony against the doctor. The nurses were steadfast in their recounting of events, maintaining a commitment to excellence, ethics, and integrity. At the hearings they pushed hard for accountability and transparency regardless of title, rank, or profession. Medical and legal authorities punished the doctor as a result of the nurses' bravery. In an event of sorrow the founding spirit of CHE poured through the hearts of these exceptional caregivers.

The terrorist attacks of September 11, 2001 sent shockwaves through CHE as they did througout the United States. Hospital staff took strength from each other, crying together, praying together, reflecting together. In addition to mutual comfort, the people of CHE received an unusual letter from William Corley. The tensions unleashed by "9-11" reached the east side of Indianapolis three weeks later when a local gas station near CHE came under media scrutiny for supposed price gouging in the aftermath of the attacks. Corley immediately wrote a letter in support of the gas station owners. "They've been an institution over here on the east side," Corley wrote to CHE staff, "They've gone out of their way many times for our people." Corley urged employees to ignore the accusations for what they were—fears born from a mindless disaster. CHE's staff would take care of one of its neighbors.

The new 21st century brought new indications of the changing neighborhoods around CHE. A new local organization formed, "Near East Area Renewal," or NEAR as it was known. The increasing number of delapidated houses led to the creation of NEAR to accelerate the renovation of run-down homes and buildings.

Within CHE, further evidence pointed to an aging patient population. The professional journal "Nursing" published an article researched at CHE; the topic was end-of-life care for the terminally ill elderly. A special presentation of other research—entitled "Geriatric Pharmacy Clinical Tutorial"—was given to staff. CHE recorded its oldest patient death since founding: 105-year-old Aarno Parma had lived and worked near CHE since immigrating from Europe's Baltic region in 1949.

Throughout 2002-2003, CHE's patients included prominent indigent cases. A poor family without insurance relied on the hospital for treatment of a child who had contracted rabies. Parents brought their quadriplegic son, an ex-felon, to the hospital for rehabilitation services; CHE welcomed him. East-side residents poured into the hospital when an 18-fold increase in influenza struck the region.

The hospital received a blow in 2003 that might have crushed the spirit of an ordinary organization. Acknowledging the population trends that continued to mark central Indiana, Community's board determined to remove the pediatric and open heart surgery programs from CHE to the North campus in Castleton. It was, in the words of one doctor, "a tough decision to take."

With new tides of worry rolling into the Ritter Avenue hospital, CHE's founding spirit showed itself again. Staff ignored diminishing resources and developed an amazing number of new programs: "Shapedown" by Robin Strahl, a children's weight-loss initiative unique to the region, combining exercise, diet, and family therapy; Meryam Cole crafted a radiology technician training strategy that attracted new employees from central Indiana; a newly-created position known as the Resource Coordination Administrator to help streamline efficiencies; and the Center for Interventional Radiology was launched, one of a handful in the nation and the only such offering in the Midwest.

Beyond these programs, CHE achieved a near-miraculous accomplishment in 2004. The cardiologists and cardiology nurses at CHE helped the hospital earn the designation of one of the "Top 100" American cardiovascular programs. One of the key reasons behind the recognition was the tireless work of nurse Susan Holbrook-Preston. Proof of her efforts came from such unlikely sources as a pair of heart surgeons from Methodist Hospital. They sent patients to the cardiovascular program and saw her and other nurses in action. They were so impressed that one of the surgeons called Corley to praise Holbrook-Preston and the entire program. If possible, the commendations from a rival hospital's surgeons may have meant even more than the lofty national ranking.

By now it was clear that CHE was the family that wouldn't quit. The hospital had taken hits from governmental and regulatory changes, hits from a declining local economy, but the people at the Ritter Avenue facility refused to give up. They worked with uncommon devotion to the welfare of patients and to the neighborhoods where they lived.

William Corley cherished their determination and resolve. The time had come, however, for a change. Something had to be done to assist CHE in its quest to survive, to serve as a bulwark of steadiness in a rapidly changing east side of Marion County. In spring 2004 Corley and the Community board agreed that a big step had to be taken.

They looked inside the organization and found an answer. They called upon a woman who had worked for thirty years at CHE along with service as a volunteer medical missionary in Cuba, Haiti, and Vietnam. She also had a hobby that might prove useful.

CHAPTER 11
Finding New From The Old, 2004-2013

Old clothes, blankets, and sheets lay in a pile. Over the years, heavy usage has worn out the fabric and frayed the stitching. Long ago, the material lost its vibrancy and color and fell out of of style. The untrained eye stares at the pile and sees a heap fit for the trash bin. The trained eye, however, sees something else. In the mess are pieces, in the pieces are potential, and in the potential is the vision of a new creation. This is the life of a quilt in the sight of a quiltmaker.

When William Corley and the board chose Anita Harden to become the next president of Community Hospital East, they unknowingly called into service a leader who was, in fact, a quilt-maker. In addition to her three decades at CHE in behaviorial health, Harden enjoyed making quilts in her spare time. She relished finding good portions of old fabric, cutting them into varying sizes and shapes, and sewing them together into a unified, colorful whole. She had the patience, the energy, the vision.

As new CEO of Community Hospital East in 2004, Harden brought more of her quilt-making skills to work than anyone knew. She had to assist her executive team and the rest of the doctors, nurses, staff, and volunteers at CHE in locating the resources of an east-side economy that continued to lag behind the rest of central Indiana. Together, in order to survive and keep the hospital strong, they would need to produce a new fabric from a struggling community.

Harden's life had important elements that enriched her selection as Corley's successor. Harden had grown up in an east side family with deep local roots. Her father had worked as a lawyer, her mother as a teacher, and each of them instilled the personal value of contributing to neighborhoods in the vicinity of the hospital. In addition, Harden's career at Community was in psychology and behavioral health, both of which had played prominent roles in the founding and early years of CHE.

The choice of Harden for the position was historic for the organization and the city. Harden was only the second African-American woman to be named CEO of a hospital in Indiana; the first was Patricia Maryland at St. Vincent Hospital a year before Harden's emergence. In addition, with William Corley elevated to CEO of Community Health Network, Harden was CHE's first chief executive whose defined role was strictly at the hospital homestead of Ritter Avenue.

In fact, Harden had spent the past several years not at Community Hospital East but at Community Hospital North. This aspect of Harden's career was a subtle asset to her in the new CEO position at Ritter Avenue. Her counterpart at Community Hospital North, Mark Moore, had been Harden's boss. Moore was one of Harden's most ardent supporters. When asked about her new role at CHE, Moore replied, "She knows the market well and can bring renewed enthusisam to the hospital." Harden's relationship with Moore and her years at North would be key factors in reducing the anxiety of people who worked at CHE.

Harden's vision was clear from the start. "The Eastside built this hospital almost a half-century ago," she announced in May 2004, "I have begun work with the mayor's office to determine what ideas and resources there are for the Eastside, and how we (CHE) can assist." Harden recognized that CHE had more than a location in eastside neighborhoods, it had a relationship with the eastside neighborhoods. This view placed the hospital squarely at the heart of two missions—caring for patients and caring for community. She wanted CHE's employees to focus themselves on both missions.

The effect on Community Hospital East were almost instantaneous. Harden publicized to city residents the current projects to renovate the lobby, train employees to act as patient-focused concierge staff, and develop an angioplasty suite for interventional radiology where, Harden noted, three of the most talented interventional radiologists in Indiana served patients at CHE. Within days of Harden's announcement, an east side branch of National City Bank donated $100,000 to CHE for improvements to the hospital's emergency department. "We appreciate the commitment the bank has made to the continued development of the East Side of Indianapolis," said a hospital spokesperson.

Harden inaugurated a round of new action at CHE. Hospital staff designed a new support group for patients suffering from Lupus, a condition that disproportionately affected African-Americans and a growing population group near CHE. A robot, four feet tall and three feet wide, delivered lab specimens to technicians for analysis. Another new program was dedicated to reducing ventilator-assisted pneumonia. Led by nurses Laurie Fish and Theresa Murray as well as respiratory therapist Dan Kidwell, the program gained significant recognition for cutting the incident rate to zero during a twelve-month span. CHE was the first site in the Network to make such an improvement, launching the hospital on an amazing five-year stretch of no cases of ventilator-assisted pneumonia.

A spirit of cheerfulness spread across the hospital. Maregatti Interiors arrived at CHE and re-designed spaces to add light, color, and style for patients and staff. The internal make-over inspired a contest for facial makeovers of six employees at Regis Hair Salon and LS Ayres retail store in Washington Square Mall. Special celebrations included honors for the passing of time: CHE celebrated anniversaries of Mary Browning, the vice president of nursing and a 15-year veteran of the hospital; Chaplain Sister Ann Matilda Holloran received honors for 50 years service at Sisters of Providence in Indianapolis; and the 100th birthday of Women's Auxiliary volunteer Hazel Pahl, creator of the hospital's "puppy pillows" for local children.

Good feelings from the hospital flowed into the community.

"Santa's Christmas Party" became a new event at CHE for children from east side homes. In warmer weather, CHE was the organizing entity behind "Family Fun Festivals" and appearances in Ellenberger Park by the Indianapolis Symphony Orchestra. The symphonic concerts became a cultural staple for the next several years on the east side.

In July 2006 the Indianapolis Symphony Orchestra was part of the fiftieth anniverary celebration of CHE's founding. The hospital sponsored a special concert that featured patriotic music, a food tent, and games. The event was planned to remind both the staff and the surrounding community that CHE was "the mother ship" of the system and an enduring resource for the east side of Indianapolis. Another event in the half-century celebration was a series of games, drawings, picnicking, and the distribution of special commemorative pens and other items in the hospital's parking lot. It was "the best fun," said Karri Amory, a radiologist.

With constant interaction between the hospital and neighborhoods, the doors of CHE never seemed to close. For the next five years, down to 2009, CHE and its community outreach director Dan Hodgkins tackled east side issues ranging from homes to education. Swinging a hammer: hospital employees banded together to build two "Habitat For Humanity" houses. Digging with shovels: CHE staff joined in a season-finale episode of "Extreme Home Makeover", an ABC-TV show, to plant 1500 trees along east-side streets and to maintain them for a year. Watering the soil: still other employees worked with Wellspring Pharmacy and the Indiana Medical Museum to plant medicinal herb gardens near Indianapolis Public School #88. Teaching and mentoring: Project Search was a CHE-based program that aided mentally- and physically-challenged high school students in training for jobs at the hospital. Directing traffic: the Near Eastside Orbiter was a public transportation vehicle used to shuttle east-side residents to CHE, shopping centers, schools, and the Boner Community Center. CHE's workforce renewed its bond with the surrounding neighborhoods.

The people of eastern Indianapolis and Marion County also enjoyed a renewal of the hospital's capacity. In 2008, as Anita Harden announced her decision to retire the following year—she had worked in health care nearly forty years—Community Hospital East offered three new centers: the Seasons Unit for Adult Behavioral Care Needs; the Joint Camp for Orthopedic Rehabilitation; and the Burn Center. Together with the Community Regional Cancer Care Radiation Oncology Treatment Center, these new features accounted for major advancements in health care for east side residents.

The final year of the decade saw a flurry of action at CHE. The Indianapolis Star promoted a special "Salute Nurses" edition in which 35-year nursing veteran Margaret Moore of CHE was honored with a "Lifetime of Compassion" award. Moore affirmed that CHE was "a great place to be a nurse" and that the hospital "respected you as a nurse. She credited Jan Bingle as a key reason for the high quality of nursing at CHE. Another CHE nurse, Lury Kutruff, won a "Patient Safety Award" from Community's Network for designing a quiet zone to decrease medical errors and increase speed of treatment for cardiac patients. Kutruff praised Dr. Glenn Bingle for his guidance. A grateful patient from Hook Rehabilation Center, Tim Hoffer, volunteered to create a special program to deliver inspirational words to current patients, assuring them as they approached tense periods of post-operative rehabilitation.

The other significant event of 2009 was the succession of Anita Harden. New Community Health Network CEO Bryan Mills and the Community board continued their strategy of hiring a successor from within the organization. They also maintained their choice of a female CEO, a practice that remained unique in health care. And whether consciously or not, they extended their selection of an organizational leader with a powerful record of civic-minded medicine.

Dr. Robin Ledyard answered their call. A native of Shelby County, forty-eight years old, and a family physician, Ledyard had taught and helped administer the Family Practice Residency Program at CHE since 1995. She was knowledgeable, friendly, and displayed an easy manner with people. Ledyard and her husband, also a physician, were life-long practicioners of health care that affected people where they worked, lived, and learned.

In the months prior to Harden's departure, Ledyard had helped design a unique school-hospital initiative. Ledyard worked to secure financial support from Community Health Foundation and, later, the federal government. As CEO, she opened the project to the public. It would prove to be one of CHE's most unique initiatives and a monument to Ledyard's understanding of the bond between families and their hospital.

The project was the Jane Pauley Community Health Center. Named in honor of national television newscaster Jane Pauley, a native of Indianapolis's east side and graduate of Warren Central High School, the project consisted of a health clinic located at Pauley's alma mater. With characteristic modesy, Pauley observed that while her name on the Center might help draw attention to it, the more meaningful and longer-lasting importance of the project was the treatment given to each incoming student and family.

The Pauley Center offered health services to not only students but also residents who lived in Warren Township. The Center's fees were calculated on a sliding schedule, including no-cost services for those who couldn't afford payment. In addition, the center provided on-site mental health services as a way to encourage holistic treatment and prevention.

The added emphasis on mental health was one of the most unique features of this unique project. Just a few years earlier, Jane Pauley had experienced a traumatic reaction to treatments of bee stings. The reaction acted as a trigger, revealing the presence of bipolar disorder in Pauley. In a decision of courage and resolve, Pauley urged Ledyard and a team at CHE to include mental health services in the Center project.

The CHE team displayed similar openness in discussions about where to locate the Center. Peggy Hinckley, Warren Township Superintendent of Schools, suggested to Ledyard and Dan Hodgkins, CHE's director of community outreach, that the Center should be placed in a Warren Township school. For the past decade CHE and Warren Township schools had worked together in partnership—a school-based health clinic had operated in a local school since the late 1990s. But the Pauley Center would be different as a stand-alone health center for residents near Warren Central High School. Hinton and Community Health Network CEO Bryan Mills concurred that the Pauley Center would welcome patients of all ages and operate at the Renaissance School next to the high school. "Our mission is to provide access to health care and improve the health of area residents," Mills stated. Hinton explained, "Healthy students are more focused on their learning, enabling them to achieve at higher levels. When families are healthy, they can focus their energy on supporting their students academic goals."

The twin decisions of the Pauley Center's location and action launched a project that quickly found success. Dr. Virginia Caine, public health director of Marion County, deemed the Center "a life preserver" to eastern Indianapolis. Caine judged the Center was the only thing standing between the area's residents and a total absence of health care. Residents and funders agreed, for within three years the Center expanded to five other schools in eastern Marion County and greater Indianapolis. A new partner, the Indiana University School of Dentistry, joined the Center to offer dental services.

The Pauley project was the latest application of ideas and values first seen in the founding of CHE, in the buckets of dollars and shovels of dirt on Indianapolis's east side of 1954-1956. The inspiration of C.P. Van Meter, Edmund Gallahue, Robert Efromyson, and Alma Bruck gained new form with the Jane Pauley Community Health Center in 2009-2012. The Pauley Centers were among the most visible benefits when CHE commissioned an economic-impact study for the region. The Pauley Centers showed the embrace between the people of eastern Marion County and their hospital.

The desire to excel on behalf of the surrounding community was seen as much at CHE's Ritter Avenue campus as it was in the Pauley Centers. The Joint Care Center and its joint replacement program grew at an amazing rate. The Joint Commission awarded a rating of excellence for the Center, while CHE's achieved a positive rating with more than 90% of its patients, many of whom were elderly and minority patients. CHE had one of the most prominent minimally invasive treatment programs for women in central Indiana with such doctors as Stuart Fraley, Michelle Murphy, Anthony Saunders, and Martina Mutove. Certification groups gave CHE a bronze medal for its organ transplant program and a silver medal for stroke treatment protocols.

The Family Medicine Residency Program, a rich part of Ledyard's background and the current pride of Dr. Clifford Knight, received formal commendation for excellence from the National Committee for Quality Assurance. This was the first such program to earn the distinction in central Indiana. In addition, both CHE and the North campus established affiliations with the nationally prestigious MD Anderson Cancer Network at Houston, Texas. And *U.S. News & World Report* ranked CHE's neurology and neurosurgery progams as 9th best in the nation.

The prominence of doctors in these achievements pointed to the continuing trait of physician excellence at CHE. Ledyard's experience as a doctor, both as a teacher and practicioner, maintained the high degree of physician pride at the Ritter Avenue campus. Indeed, Ledyard was a key factor in the cohesion of the physician network at CHE. She, her executive team, and departmental leaders across the organization devoted time and energy to upholding strong relationships with and among doctors connected to the hospital.

In fall 2013, CHE was part of a re-organization effort within the Community Health Network. Robin Ledyard moved into a formal leadership role of as senior vice president of Community's Physician Network, one of the largest in Indiana. Scott Teffeteller became CHE's new chief executive officer. Teffeteller was a veteran hospital executive, having been CEO at Union Hospital in Terre Haute, Indiana. He also had extensive service in the for-profit hospital organization, Hospital Corporation of America.

The executive team he inherited from Ledyard was sound and talented. Among them, Paige Dooley was chief nursing officer, a revered leader in her own right, inspiring and motivating to all who knew her. It was hard not to feel uplifted by her energy. Don Ziperman possessed medical knowledge that spanned decades. With twinkling eyes and a wry smile, Ziperman brought a unique blend of steadiness, wit, and an innovative curiosity to his work as chief medical officer. Jason Landis, as chief financial officer, was modest, disarming, unassuming, and blessed with rock-solid integrity; he was an expert in the financial workings of the hospital. Julie Ertel exuded compassion, warmth, experience, and a sense of calling as vice president of quality. Dooley, Ziperman, Landis, Ertel, and others in key management positions had contributed to the onset of fourteen different performance improvement programs across the hospital on Ritter Avenue by the time of Teffeteller's arrival.

The executive team embodied the rest of the hospital's workforce. Long-standing experience on Ritter Avenue, a keen insight into the connection between the hospital and neighborhoods, and a purposeful choice in continuing with CHE, all of these traits made the executive team and the rest of the staff and volunteers similar parts of the same whole.

But like William Corley years before, Teffeteller was the stranger, the outsider, the new face at the family door. He also happened to be just the right combination of cheerleader and river-boat gambler.

CHAPTER 12
Re-Founding, 2014-2018

The stranger at the door wasn't entirely out of place. In one important way, Scott Teffeteller embodied the return of the native at Community Hospital East.

In leadership style, he resembled Allen Hicks. He was jovial, encouraging, gregarious, optimistic—quick to smile, extend a hand, and say hello. He added to this Hicks-like demeanor a strong dose of market savvy with the slightest hint of a gambler ready to toss the dice. And Teffeteller wasn't bashful about setting the sights of Community Hospital on big things. The dice were rolled.

Big things weren't exactly visible at that moment. The mood at CHE was rather downcast after receiving word that one of the hospital's long-time capacities, the Hook Rehabilitative Center, would be relocated to the North campus. It was another move that reminded staff of the obvious economic difficulties of the east side. Feelings of worry drifted along Ritter Avenue.

Nevertheless, Teffeteller and his immediate team began discussions of two hopeful projects. Indiana legislators added new rules to the existing law for emergency medical services. At the same time, heavy neighborhood use of these services—the number of CHE emergency-room visits had risen 62% over a decade—left Teffeteller's team with the clear need to strengthen the emergency department. The team agreed on a goal: gaining designation as a "Level III Trauma Center" by the American College of Surgeons. They commenced a months-long effort to craft and gather the necessary documentation and informed the State Superintendent of Health of their intentions.

In addition to the pursuit of a new emergency designation, the team tackled the stark reality of the walls around them. Every man, woman, and child who entered CHE saw the evidence of an aging hospital. The family home was tired. Portable heaters operated in the winter to keep some of the pipes from freezing. In periods of intense rain, leaks might drip from spots in the roof. The colors were dreary and could no longer be improved with another coat of paint or layer of wallpaper. The answer was obvious. Either make major upgrades or risk losing patients, staff, and volunteers too disenchanted to continue with the hospital. The executive team started scribbling their estimates on renovations, the cost, layout, timeline, and more.

This was where newcomer Teffeteller played a key role. He urged the team to go for more, to think about an entirely new hospital that, in the long run, would likely cost less than a renovation program. This was a startling proposal; the notion of "total hospital replacement" took the team aback. But as days and weeks passed, the team grew more comfortable and confident with the idea and a consensus developed around the concept of a new hospital.

The course of this shift in thinking was one of the most important moments in the history of CHE. The context told the story.

It was a long way from the mid-1950s. Gone were the nickels, dimes, and dollars collected in cans and buckets. Gone was the harnessing of a section of a city, indeed the entire city itself, to raise money and spread the word. Gone were the fund-raising dances, the factory lunch-room presentations, and the out-of-town celebrities. And gone was the thought of a single hospital rising from the wetlands and woodlots. But in a real way, the idea of Community Health Network spending millions and millions of dollars on a state-of-the-art hospital where the original Community Hospital had stood—that was just as hard to fathom, just as hard to envision, in the late 2010s as was the founding in the early 1950s.

The obstruction to the vision wasn't in going from nothing to something, as it was decades earlier. Teffeteller's team already had something in place—a sizeable organization with established procedures, relationships, resources, and the rest. Ironically, however, that fact presented a problem of its own. There could be difficulty in trying new approaches or seeking new changes. The extent of so much pre-existence—of rules, attitudes, expectations, assumptions, limitations, and so on—was a barrier that had to be overcome by Teffeteller's team.

An added barrier for the executive team was the economy of the east side. Unlike the upswing of the early 1950s, the east side was now in economic lethargy of a quarter-century duration. Founding drew a large part of its energy from the rising prosperity of the eastern Marion County. Donations had been a vibrant element of local support and community ownership, and tracking the growing levels of donations had built tangible excitement around the concept of a hospital. Momentum for re-founding would have to come from something else.

Amazingly, the executive team uncovered a source for re-founding's momentum. It was in CHE's spirit of itself. They felt it and acted on it. The vast majority of the hospital's volunteers and staff—including most of the executive team—had endured a lot together on Ritter Avenue. They knew who they were and what the hospital was. They were the lastest generation of the founding hospital. Only one hospital in the Network had been first and it was them, it was theirs to protect. And being where they were in the city, burdens had fallen on them in all shapes and sizes. Out of these common experiences came a deep sense of resilience. They had survived and gained strength as a unit and a family, and they perceived a clear responsibility for the people and places around them.

This was the spirit that formed the vision of re-founding. No one else of similar magnitude on the east side had the choice between renovation and total rebuilding. No one else was the first hospital. No one else had worked so hard to keep health care fully open to the people who lived here. The neighborhoods of the east side were depending on them. Teffeteller's executive team wasn't about to let them down. The more they ruminated on the plan to rebuild, the more excited they became. The spirit caught life.

In April 2014 the team finalized the proposal for a new hospital and submitted it to Network CEO Bryan Mills—himself a veteran of CHE from the start of his career—and the Community board of directors. On Thursday, May 14, 2014, approval was granted for a $175 million project to build a new hospital on Ritter Avenue. The target date for the first phase of opening would be fall 2018.

Like the founding of the mid-1950s, a series of ceremonies marked the re-founding decision to construct the hospital building from scratch. The ceremonies spanned spring 2014 to summer 2015.

For the public announcement of May 14, 2015, Network CEO Bryan Mills addressed members of the local media and well-wishers. Lean, soft-spoken, and with a manner of genuine sincerity, Mills emphasized the movement of events. He stated that the first decision of renovation had given way to a concept of greater value and worth. Under the previous plan, Mills asserted that "we were spending a whole lot on infrastructure." Now, Mills explained, "We have a better project and we can do more for the Eastside and make that a destination place for the Eastside."

Mills's remarks traced a fascinating journey for CHE. In the founding, the flow of investment was from the area and neighborhoods to the newly emerging hospital. In Mills's remarks of re-founding, the flow was reversed, from the Network and existing hospital to the area and neighborhoods as a sign of re-emergence. CHE had become one of the pillars of the east side's economy, society, culture, education, and quality of life. First there was birth of the building from the neighborhoods. Now it was re-birth of the neighborhoods from the building.

In addition to Mills's speech, Indiana State Senator Patricia Miller offered insights to the audience on May 14. Her comments, while few, were poignant, a blend of humility and authenticity, and touched one of the deepest layers of the event.

Miller was among the most respected members of the Indiana legislature. Known for practicality and common sense in a volatile statehouse, Miller had first worked at CHE as a nurse prior to entering politics. Miller was a living example of CHE's organic connection to the region. Miller told the group on May 14 that as happy as she was with the Network's decision to build a new hospital on Ritter Avenue, she was also somewhat saddened. "You're tearing down some of my history," she said. Every CHE employee of numerous years—and there were scores of them either in the crowd or back at the bedside—knew exactly how she felt. They were beginning the long process of saying goodbye to the old family homestead.

Another important ceremony was on August 19, 2015 with the formal ground-breaking of the new building. On a hot day, fourteen guests gathered under a tent to dig a shovelful of dirt, a symbol that construction had begun. Indianapolis Mayor Greg Ballard, Indiana Hospital Association President Doug Leonard, and CHE chief executive officer Scott Teffeteller were among the participants. Members of Teffeteller's executive team were there, too, Dr. John Kunzer, Jason Landis, Allen Wilson, Paige Dooley, and Dr. Don Ziperman. In a twist of fate mindful of Shakespeare, Ziperman's thoughts ran to Dr. C.P. Van Meter, one of the founding physicians of the mid-1950s and a man who had walked this ground when raccoons, rabbits, squirrels, and frogs were the residents. Van Meter had been Ziperman's father-in-law.

Network CEO Bryan Mills again shared his thoughts to the assembled crowd. This time, however, Mills wasn't thinking strictly about the funds or about the project as a target of payment. Instead, the nature of ground-breaking could be heard in his remarks. "Community has a rich heritage on the east side of Indianapolis," he said. He grew even more emphatic as his speech went on. "This new hospital," Mills continued, "means we will remain firmly rooted where our story began nearly sixty years ago." Rich and rooted, story and sixty, these were words that struck at the heart of CHE's identity by this point in the 21st century. Mills emphasized the broader impact of the recent decision: "The changes coming to the Community East campus reflect the need to focus on patient well-being, while providing economic stability and community benefits to local neighborhoods." Mills's statement leaned forward, toward a future of coming changes for both the hospital and the neighborhoods.

Scott Teffeteller completed the event's roster of speakers. Attempting to contain emotion—the words floating just above an inner sense of gratefulness—Teffeteller picked up on Mills's reference to the future. "The end result," he stated, "is a campus that can create innovative strategies and handle the ever-changing trends in health care." The Twin Towers behind him bore the scars of those volatile trends. Soon, the Towers and their scars would exist only in photographs.

The final ceremony came in summer 2016. A few months prior, Indiana Governor Mike Pence announced the decision to build a state-funded $120 million mental health facility. Moving with astonishing speed, Teffeteller and his executive team along with Mills and the Community board secured approval from state officials to locate the new facility at Ritter Avenue, next to the planned site for the new CHE. The Neuro-Diagnostic Institute and Advanced Treatment Center would have capacity for 1500 patients annually, including forty-two beds for children and adolescents. The combined investment in the CHE and NDI buildings exceeded any east side projects in the past several decades.

On August 22, 2016 Community's leaders gathered for the groundbreaking celebration of the Neuro-Diagnostic Center. Like the ceremony in 1954, this event was affected by American presidential politics. The difference was that Governor Mike Pence—who was scheduled to deliver a speech at the Ritter Avenue site—was suddenly called away. Pence had been chosen as the vice presidential nominee on the presidential ticket of Republican Presidential nominee Donald Trump. Trump and Pence made an unexpected visit to storm-ravaged Baton Rouge, Louisiana.

Filling in for Pence at CHE's ceremony was Lieutenant Governor Eric Holcomb, accompanied by Indiana State Senator Luke Kenley. Holcomb expressed well-wishes from Pence. He emphasized the collaboration of Hoosiers across the levels of government in bringing the proposal to life next to CHE. Pence and Holcomb didn't realize it, but their remarks were strikingly similar in theme to those offered in more elaborate form by President Eisenhower and Vice President Nixon.

Dr. John Wernert, Secretary of Indiana's Family and Social Services Administration, and Community Network CEO Bryan Mills followed Holcomb. Wernert described the Neuro-Diagnostic Center as a potential national best-practice in mental health treatment.

Mills linked the new center to "the vision for behavioral health care that we developed here at Community." Mills's statement was a quiet invocation of the legacy of the early 1950s and the role of Edward Gallahue in the founding of Community. With the joining of the goal of a national best practice to the heritage of Community Hospital's founding, Gallahue's shadow rested approvingly over the new Neuro-Diagnostic Center project.

As buildings go, the construction of the new CHE required the deconstruction of the old CHE. Two of the existing buildings were torn down during spring and summer 2016. CHE's leader in facilities management, Keith Smith, observed that the old buildings were made of excellent materials. "Great integrity in those buildings," Smith noted. Truer words were never spoken.

During this period, CHE's past, present, and future were merged in a unique event. The founding's time capsule—the copper box of 1955—had been unearthed several years before by Terry Northern, a project manager with expertise in building design. Northern reburied it in a courtyard, marked by a small stone slab. Employees quickly forgot where the markers were and what they represented. In late April 2016, with CHE employees assuming the box was lost, construction crews dug up both the copper box and a second box filled with items from 1991. News of the discovery rocketed around the hospital.

The two containers were opened to much fanfare, a crowd of employees and volunteers having gathered in the CHE lobby with local media looking on. Scott Teffeteller and Paige Dooley presided over the event. Volunteer Lucille Loutner helped unpack the containers. Most of the people in the audience were older and had a long history with the hospital. Amid smiles and excited chatter, they looked at the items inside—newspapers, medical instruments, marketing materials, photographs, the vial of polio vaccine, among other things. As the items were held up and then laid out on tables, murmurs of memories filled the lobby. Observers shared brief stories with each other. After a half-hour or so, one by one the people in attendance returned to their jobs, their cars, their offices and departments, their lives in the vicinity of Ritter Avenue.

By July 2016, work had commenced on the new patient tower

of CHE, the core of the future building. The hospital's internal website monitored the progress of the building program on a daily basis. Beyond the visible changes in construction, the lives of every employee, patient, and volunteer of the hospital reflected the reality of construction. They adjusted their routines of parking, patient care, staffing, and the comings-and-goings of patients and their families. As 2017 turned to 2018, everyone saw evidence of the new building, first in the excavated foundation, and then in the steel frame, the concrete, the outer walls, and more. A new era at Community Hospital East came into view.

The new CHE would feature the latest capacities of 21st century health care. The $175 million-dollar building would encompass a totally new emergency department, medical imaging, delivery rooms, surgical rooms, and patient rooms. A pneumatic tube system promised to deliver lab specimens at unrivaled speeds. The most modern food service, staffing centers, and patient waiting areas would be available. An emphasis would be returned to the importance of gathering places for professional staff. Finally, a powerful cellular tower would be located in the center of the campus. The tower would provide communication services to not only the hospital campus but to large swaths of eastern Indianapolis.

CHE's Keith Smith was a vital leader in the massive construction project. He and his facilities team were diligent in design and planning. They collaborated with clinical staff and executives to ensure that the new hospital aligned smoothly with the new NDI building. They ensured that the complex sequencing of construction did not cause chaos with existing demands of patient care. Using local workers from the east side whenever possible and paying extra attention to external aesthetics, they maintained excellent relations with nearby residents and businesses.

Chief Operating Officer Suzanne Kohler was one of the leaders of a strategy to prepare all employees for the shifting into the new building. Her co-leader was Chief Nursing Officer Paige Dooley, recent recipient of the prestigious "Health Care Heros" award sponsored by the Indianapolis Business Journal.

Kohler and Dooley's challenges were many, including moving

employees familiar with the circular work patterns of the Twin Towers and its multiple points of access into an unfamiliar setting of linear work flows and more centralized controls. In spring 2016 they developed "Transitions Operating Plan Team", the TOP Team. Using week-long retreats, regular follow-up meetings, targeted team goals, and a steady stream of communication, Kohler, Dooley, and the TOP Team outlined the steps needed to provide seamless care to patients in the new buildings. Much of the activity revolved around technology and personalized care. Koehler praised the invaluable role of frontline staff's crucial role in defining the best practices needed for the new building.

Koehler was a recent arrival at CHE, having started on Teffeteller's executive team in fall 2016. She immediately realized that the utmost priority was to prevent the new buildings from obliterating the culture and identity of CHE. She sensed that the hospital's achievements were sadly overlooked, that CHE "was the best-kept secret of the city." Koehler asserted that the new campus, the new East, would by 2020 "harken back to the initial campus developed here in light of the needs expressed by the people of the near east side of the city. It will remain an anchoring institution for a long, long time."

Koehler's anchor was a fact. Typical was the view of newly hired nurse Caleb Thompson who stated that "from day one at Community Hospital East, I've felt like part of a family." He listed the family ways seen in the hospital's hallways—employees greeting each other, knowing one another's name, taking the time to do something extra for colleagues, and more. Thompson perceived a two-step effect where the mutual caring among staff translated into a devotional caring of patients. Thompson observed, "I hope the growth at East doesn't change the culture there. It's something special and something to be held dear." This was the anchor Koehler wanted to maintain.

While the TOP Team readied their colleagues for the new building, the hard work of daily health care continued at CHE. In January 2017 CHE became the home site of the Shelbourne Clinic. The clinic was the first center in Indiana meant specifically for treatment of knee injuries. Dr. Don Shelbourne had launched his clinic in 2004 and was now relocating it at Ritter Avenue in a newly renovated space. The site soon became busy with the many patients of Shelbourne Clinic.

The CHE Auxiliary was as vibrant as ever. For the first time, volunteers served in the neo-natal intensive care unit, the NICU. They made bright-colored blankets for the unit and cuddled babies whose mothers were struggling with addictions. Auxiliary members relished their time in the NICU, with volunteers filling three shifts of service. Also, members raised $25,000 for a scholarship in honor of deceased volunteer Margaret Southworth who had trained Judy Moran, a member of the Auxiliary and its representative on the patient advisory board. Southworth's family directed the scholarship would be used for a college student majoring in nursing or another healthcare field.

The sorrow that Auxiliary volunteers saw in the NICU was part of a bigger pattern documented in CHE research. An innovative analysis of the vicinity around the hospital produced a stunning conclusion. Forty percent of the local population was on Medicaid and, shockingly, the life expectancy of residents was almost thirteen years less than people living in the more affluent northside of Indianapolis. CHE staff reported local outbreak of a national problem—opiods. Opiate drugs were found in one of every five babies born at the hospital in the first half of 2016. Doctors and nurses at CHE worked desperately to treat both mothers and infants for the effects of addiction.

Dr. John Kunzer, medical director, led a hospital-wide effort to secure a large federal grant to understand population health in eastern Indianapolis. Kunzer's "Community Collaboration" initiative consisted of screening for social factors in health care, wider use of medical screenings, and intense development of local leaders to facilitate ties between the hospital and residents. Kunzer was a physician leader whose modest demeanor and selfless style strengthened the willingness of east-side citizens and community organizations to enhance their relationship with CHE. CHE received the grant and began in early 2018 to implement "Community Collaboration." The biggest part of Kunzer's initiative would be executed later in 2018, well-timed with the schedule to open the new campus.

There was one more decision to be made.

Somewhere at CHE sat a box. The box was a hard shell, made to survive the effects of weather and of burial. Nothing was inside. It was empty.

This was the Time Capsule of 2018, soon to hold the treasures of the New East, as it was now commonly called. The people and neighborhoods of Community Hospital East on Ritter Avenue would need to decide what to put in the box. Surely the latest medical gadgets and marketing materials will number among the items. And yet the box will include as well some symbol of the spirit, the seed, that was also planted in the ground back all those years ago.

The people will tend it now as they tended it then.

April 1954, the future site of Community Hospital East. Among other things, state and city officials hoped that new buildings on sites like this would reduce the amount of trash which, they feared, might otherwise accelerate the outbreak of fire during a hydrogen-bomb attack.

In 1954, a work crew conducts soil testing in the acreage near Ritter Avenue and 16th Street. Their work was a key step prior to digging the foundation of the future Community Hospital East.

Western Electric employees at a hospital fund-raising revent. From paychecks and pocketbooks and piggy banks, residents of eastern Indianapolis and Marion County offered their money to build the community's hospital.

Carl Dorah, left, greets Jean Hersholt at the Indianapolis airport. Hersholt was a keynote speaker for a fund-raising dinner in 1954. He was nationally known for the title role in the radio drama, Dr. Christian. Hersholt was so trusted as an entertainer that he received fan letters asking for medical advice.

Denison Parking Service Chief Executive Officer William Griffith gives a speech during the fund-raising campaign. Willis Conner, Jr is seated next to him. Griffith and Conner brought extensive experience in business and community leadership to the effort.

Indianapolis Power & Light display during the fund-raising campaign. Community Hospital East is at the center of the display because of its prominence as an expression of community spirit.

A television was one of the most popular prizes to reward those who collected money for the community's hospital.

Conducted by Fabien Sevitzky, the Indianapolis Symphony Orchestra performed at fund-raising activities that financed the building of Community Hospital East. Sevitzky and the ISO had made recordings for RCA Victor and Capitol Records.

An Indianapolis jazz band performs for RCA employees at a fund-raising event. Popular music was an important part of fund-raising efforts.

William Book of the Indianapolis Chamber of Commerce at a V For Victory dinner during the fund-raising campaign. The slogan harkened back to local drives for donations of money and items during World War II.

You are invited :

Ground Breaking Ceremonies

COMMUNITY HOSPITAL, INC.
16th Street & Ritter Avenue
Thursday 3:10 p.m. Sept. 23

*Made possible through gifts
to the*

INDIANAPOLIS HOSPITAL DEVELOPMENT FUND

This is your program...please bring it to the ground breaking ceremonies

Invitation to the Ground-Breaking Ceremony

Community Hospital
of Indianapolis, Inc.

The Invitation

US Vice-President Richard Nixon arrives to participate in the Ground-Breaking Ceremony, September 1954. Nixon's staff and local police argued over the security concerns of allowing the Vice-President to ride in a convertible.

Motorcade arrived at the Ground-Breaking Ceremony in September 1954. It was a day long remembered in eastern Marion County.

Charles Lynn, Vice-President of Eli Lilly and Company, served as master of ceremonies at the Ground-Breaking Ceremony. Lynn was especially interested in including people of diverse backgrounds in the new hospital.

Left to right, Vice President Richard Nixon, Willis Conner, Jr, Bill Shirley, and Rev. Monsignor Henry Dugan at the opening prayer of the Ground-Breaking Ceremony. For many, the occasion was a prayer already answered.

Bill Shirley performing a solo at the Ground-Breaking Ceremony in September 1954. Born in Indianapolis, Shirley was a popular radio singer and performer.

Vice President Richard Nixon at the Ground-Breaking Ceremony. Nixon's speech touched on significant political issues.

Another view of the Ground-Breaking Ceremony. The crowd awaits the arrival of Vice-President Richard Nixon.

More of the Ground-Breaking Ceremony festivities. A holiday atmosphere surrounded the event on a gorgeous autumn day.

Another CHE hospital expansion recognized and celebrated.

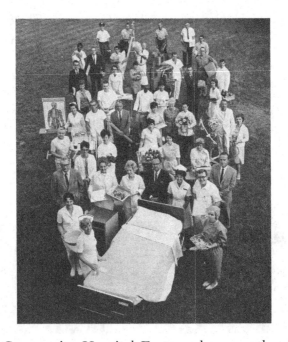

Forty-five Community Hospital East employees gather in 1968 to represent the wide array of services offered at the hospital. They didn't know that soon another event, the murder of Martin Luther King Jr, would also test the mettle of their organization.

Clarice White was one of the most popular workers to serve on Community Hospital East's Telecare program in 1973. Colleagues knew she would brave the worst weather in order to arrive at her post at the hospital.

Left to right, Governor Otis Bowen, Elke Finch, Bud Hook, and Allen Hicks, in 1974. Bowen and Hook were two of the most recognizable leaders in Indiana.

In 1976 Alys Kline receives the first 20-year employee award at Community Hospital East from Allen Hicks, Chief Executive Officer. Kline was a widely respected leader throughout the hospital.

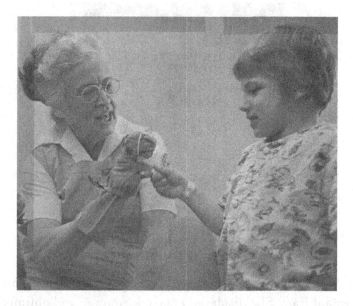

Women's Auxiliary volunteer Lucille Latz shows a puppet to patient Jamie Meyer in 1976. The volunteers were a vital bridge between the hospital and the community.

Drs. Robert Edmands and John Mercho discuss a case. Drs. Mercho and H.A. Roushdi began the cardiovascular surgical program at Community Hospital East. The program was among the most important break-throughs at the hospital.

Bonnie Stehle, the first cardiovascular surgical patient at Community
Hospital East. She displayed amazing courage and optimism.

Glenn Bingle, Ph.D, Medical Education Director, congratulates David
Josephson, M.D., for receiving the 1980 Physician of the Year Award
at Community Hospital East. Dr. Bingle was a devoted champion of
both excellence and innovation in eduation. Dr. Josephson embodied
the prominence of continuous learning in Community's physicians.

Left to right, Lillian Danner, Dr. Glenn Bingle, and Beulah Smith, National Volunteer Week, 1982. Volunteer Week was always a special time at Community Hospital East.

Image 06: Martha Biedelman with Sheila Hotstetter in the Resource Center, 1989. The Resource Center was a busy place at Community Hospital East.

The balloon was a part of the celebration in 1990 of Community Hospital East's building expansion.

left to right, Boris Meditch, President of National Wholesale Grocery; Gene Step, Chief Financial Officer at Eli Lilly and Company; and William Corley, Chief Executive Officer, CHE

William Dyer, Jr, the only original member of Community Hospital East's Board of Directors who was still living in 1991. Dyer talks with William Corley, President and CEO of Community and Kathryn Betler, chairwoman of the board of the Community Foundation. Dyer was a living connection to the people who founded the hospital.

The first Physician-Vendor-Employee Basketball tournament. 1991. The game illustrated the importance of personal relationships in the functioning of Community Hospital East.

Joyce Eaton, R.N., Director of Patient Care Services, Women's and Children's Services; Trudy Christner, R.N., Nurse Manager, Pediatrics; Alice Staleup, volunteer; Maxine Mincer, Women's Auxiliary, President; Pat Tubbs, R.N., Pediatrics. They tour the renovated pediatrics, the result of donations from hospital employees and volunteers in 1991.

Daniel Neufelder, Executive Vice President and Chief Operating Officer; Russell Judd, M.D., and Chief of Staff; John Lowe, M.D., and President-elect; and John Nunshower, M.D., Secretary-Treasurer, mark the opening of the hospital courtyard in 1991. The space was funded by a gift from the Medical Staff of Community Hospital and symbolized the close relationship between physicians and the hospital.

Jean Fee, Richard Finch, and Elke Finch. Elke Finch, born without a left leg and left arm, was a long-time recipient of support from the Women's Auxiliary.

Dr. Paul Kirkhoff, one of the first physicians at Community Hospital East. He received a special award in 2000 for fifty years of medical service. Dr. Kirkhoff was truly a pioneer of medical care in eastern Indianapolis.

The first formal leader of the hospital, Wilbur McLin (chief executive, 1955-1971) provided a firm and steady hand as CHE grew from the soil of eastern Marion County and the eastside of Indianapolis. He blended a thirst for organizational growth and innovation with a devotion to local engagement.

A stranger to none and a friend to all, Allen Hicks (chief executive, 1972-1983) injected an invaluable zeal and enthusiasm into the culture of CHE. The last place where Hicks could be found was in his office; he was usually meeting with employees or key leaders in the city, state, and nation.

Disciplined, organized, and focused, William Corley (chief executive, 1985-2003) confronted the uncharted waters of moving the hospital into a defined health system across metropolitan Indianapolis. Relying on Corley's deep knowledge of systemic change, CHE adapted to meet the challenges of a dawning new century.

Anita Harden (chief executive, 2004-2008) combined a wide-ranging background of education and experience in nursing, behaviorial health, and business administration. She reinvigorated Community's sense of its commitment to local health accessibility and a spirit of excellence. She skillfully guided CHE through a period of massive community change.

Dr. Robin Ledyard (chief executive, 2009-2013) brought a unique blend of medical expertise and community-based patient care to her years at the helm of CHE. The Jane Pauley Community Health Center, which she helped develop, typified Ledyard's passion for real medical excellence across diverse communities.

Blessed with the charm and verve of a riverboat gambler, Scott Teffeteller (chief executive, 2013-2018) was the prime first mover of the vision of the new CHE. His willingness to take risks played a key role in making the new campus one of the biggest local investments in the history of eastern Marion County.

Paige Dooley (chief executive, 2019-) was widely renowned for incomparable care-giving and leadership as a nurse and administrator. She sparked a renewal of intensive connections--bedside and curbside alike--between the hospital's employees and both patients and patients' families. Her example inspired new approaches to CHE's role in the renewed eastern Indianapolis and Marion County.